PHYTOCHEMICALS FROM PLANTS HEALTH BENEFITS

DR. HILAL AHMAD PUNOO

Dedicated to all the scholars and readers

Contents

FOREWORD

I'm delighted to write this preface since I've known Dr. Hilal Ahmad Punoo for quite some time. Furthermore, I feel he has conducted sound research with several consequences, particularly in the science realm.

Dr. Hilal Ahmad Punoo's work on "Phytochemicals From Plants: Health Benefits" is an excellent piece of work that is still relevant in today's world. He has thoroughly researched the issue of phtochemicals from a variety of perspectives that might be valuable to a variety of stakeholders.

Furthermore, he has based his research on a significant theory, which gives the research greater weight.

Dr. P.K. Singh
Associate Professor
Punjab Agricultural University
Ludhina, Punjab

PREFACE

The phytochemical category covers substances that are considered as necessary nutrients, meaning they are found naturally in plants and are needed for proper physiological activities, hence they must be received from human food. Although there is limited research on specific phytochemicals in foods and their effects on disease risk, there is enough evidence—mostly from studies looking at the link between foods high in phytochemicals and disease risk—to strongly suggest that eating foods and beverages high in these compounds may help prevent disease. Researchers discovered that phytochemicals have the ability to stimulate the immune system, prevent toxic substances in the diet from becoming carcinogenic, reduce inflammation, prevent DNA damage and aid DNA repair, reduce oxidative damage to cells, slow cancer cell growth, cause damaged cells to self-destruct (apoptosis) before they can reproduce, help regulate intracellular signalling of hormones and gene expression, and activate insulin receptors. According to research, persons who consume the recommended amount of fruits and vegetables have much greater phytochemical intakes. This book discusses phytochemicals and their potential health advantages. It gives details on antioxidants derived from phytochemicals that have health advantages.

Thus, it is essential to study this phenomenon in detail, especially the benefits associated with it. This book is an important endeavour to study phytochemicals and its associated factors.

Dr. Hilal Ahmad Punoo

Acknowledgements

I thank the Almighty that has showered me with blessing and grace to complete this piece of work.

I am indeed grateful to Mr. Khurshid Ahmad, Junior Assistant in Food Science and Technology university of Kashmir for guiding me in typing the manuscript diligently and accurately. Thanks are due to all my students (past and present), friends and well-wishers for their continued support in this endeavor.

I would also like to express my gratefulness for my parents for their support and love.

Dr. Hilal Ahmad Punoo

PROLOGUE

Phytochemicals are chemical compounds produced by plants, generally to help them resist fungi, bacteria and plant virus infections, and consumption by insects and other animals. Phytochemicals are chemicals of plant origin. Phytochemicals are chemicals produced by plants through primary or secondary metabolism. They generally have biological activity in the plant host and play a role in plant growth or defence against competitors, pathogens, or predators. Phytochemicals under research can be classified into major categories, such as carotenoids and polyphenols, which include phenolic acids, flavonoids, stilbenes or lignans. Flavonoids can be further divided into groups based on their similar chemical structure, such as anthocyanins, flavones, flavanones, isoflavones, and flavanols. Flavanols are further classified as catechins, epicatechins, and proanthocyanidins. In total, over 25,000 phytochemicals have been discovered, and in most cases, these phytochemicals are concentrated in colourful parts of the plants like fruits, vegetables, nuts, legumes, and whole grains. Phytochemists study phytochemicals by first extracting and isolating compounds from the original plant, followed by defining their structure or testing in laboratory model systems, such as in vitro studies using cell lines or in vivo studies using laboratory animals. Challenges in that field include isolating specific compounds and determining their structures, which are often complex, and identifying what specific phytochemical is primarily responsible for any given biological activity. The phytochemical category includes compounds recognized as essential nutrients, which are naturally contained in plants and are required for normal physiological functions, so must be obtained from the diet of humans. Non-digestible dietary fibres from plant foods, often considered a phytochemical, are now generally regarded as a nutrient group having approved health claims for reducing the risk of some types of cancer and coronary heart disease. Eating a diet high in fruits, vegetables, grains, legumes and plant-based beverages has long-term health benefits. Research on specific phytochemicals in foods and their effects on disease risk is limited, but there's enough evidence—mostly from looking at the association between foods rich in phytochemicals and disease risk—to strongly suggest that consuming foods and beverages rich in these compounds may help prevent disease. However, it isn't known whether the health benefits are the result of individual phytochemicals, the interaction of various phytochemicals, the fibre content of plant foods, or the interaction of phytochemicals and the vitamins and minerals found in the same foods. There's evidence to suggest that consuming foods rich in phytochemicals may reduce the risk of cardiovascular disease. The consumption of fruits, vegetables, and whole grains, as well as dietary patterns such as the Mediterranean diet that emphasize these foods, have been associated with a reduced risk of several types of cancer, including breast, lung, and colon. Research suggests that phytochemical-rich foods may directly decrease the risk of type 2 diabetes, most likely by reducing inflammation and improving insulin sensitivity, and indirectly by preventing weight gain, the most important risk factor of the disease. Researchers have found that phytochemicals have the potential to stimulate the immune system, prevent toxic substances in the diet from becoming carcinogenic, reduce inflammation, prevent DNA damage and aid DNA repair, reduce oxidative damage to cells, slow the growth rate of cancer cells, trigger damaged cells to self-destruct (apoptosis) before they can reproduce, help regulate intracellular signalling of hormones and gene expression, and activate insulin receptors. While the associations found regarding a diet rich in fruits, vegetables, tea, whole grains, and other plant foods are consistent and strong, they don't demonstrate a clear cause and effect relationship. However, experts such as the 2010 Dietary Guidelines for Americans Committee and the American Institute for Cancer Research agree that consuming a variety of plant-based foods is important for health. Research shows that those who meet the recommendations for fruit and vegetable consumption have considerably higher intakes of phytochemicals.

This book provides information about phytochemicals and their health benefits. It provides information about antioxidants from phytochemicals with health benefits. It provides information about phytochemicals from soy plant and their health benefits. It also provides information about the medicinal importance of phytochemicals. I hope this book will be useful to B.Sc, M.Sc students and researchers studying Food Technology, Human Nutrition, Agriculture and Dietetics.

I
Phytochemicals

1. Phytochemicals literally mean "plant chemicals." Scientists have identified thousands of different phytochemicals, found in vegetables, fruits, beans, whole grains, nuts and seeds. Eating lots of plant foods rich in phytochemicals may help to prevent at least one in every five cases of cancer, as well as other serious ailments such as heart disease.

How Do Phytochemicals Help Prevent Diseases?

- Stimulate the immune system, the body's defence against viruses, bacteria and other disease-causing agents.
- Block the potential for carcinogens (cancer-causing substances) to be formed in the body from substances we eat, drink and absorb from the environment.
- Reduce oxidation, the damage to cells that occurs with ageing and exposure to pollution. Oxidation, caused by molecules called "free radicals," can cause abnormalities in cells that may eventually lead to cancer.
- Slow the growth rate of cancer cells.
- Reduce inflammation that provides a setting favourable for cancer growth.
- Trigger death (a process known as apoptosis) of damaged cells that may be precursors to cancer
- Prevent DNA damage and help with DNA repair mechanisms.
- Help to regulate hormones, such as estrogen and insulin. Excess levels of these hormones are linked with an increased risk for breast and colon cancer.

೧

2. Colour of phytochemicals

• 2 •

Red

Carotenoids

- Flavonoids
- Polyphenols
- Terpenes

White

- Flavonoids
- Inositol
- Isoflavones

Blue/Purple

- Flavonoids
- Polyphenols

Green

- Carotenoids
- Flavonoids
- Indoles
- Glucosinolates
- Isothiocyanates

Yellow/Orange

- Carotenoids
- Flavonoids
- Polyphenols
- Terpenes

ॐ

3. Types of Phytochemicals

Phytochemical(s)

I. Carotenoids

- beta-carotene
- lycopene
- lutein
- zeaxanthin

Plant Source

Red, orange and green fruits and vegetables include broccoli, carrots, cooked tomatoes, leafy greens, sweet potatoes, winter squash, apricots, cantaloupe, oranges and watermelon.

Possible Benefits

May inhibit cancer cell growth, work as antioxidants and improve immune response.

ii. Flavonoids

- anthocyanins
- quercetin

Plant Source

Apples, citrus fruits, onions, soybeans and soy products (tofu, soy milk, edamame, etc.), coffee and tea.

Possible Benefits

May inhibit inflammation and tumour growth; may aid immunity and boost production of detoxifying enzymes in the body.

iii. Indoles and Glucosinolates

- sulforaphane

Plant Source

Cruciferous vegetables (broccoli, cabbage, collard greens, kale, cauliflower and Brussels sprouts).

Possible Benefits

May induce detoxification of carcinogens, limit production of cancer-related hormones, block carcinogens and prevent tumour growth.

iv. Inositol

- phytic acid

Plant Source

Bran from corn, oats, rice rye and wheat, nuts, soybeans and soy products (tofu, soy milk, edamame, etc.).

Possible Benefits

May retard cell growth and work as an antioxidant.

v. Isoflavones

- daidzein
- genistein

Plant Source

Soybeans and soy products (tofu, soy milk, edamame, etc.).

Possible Benefits

May inhibit tumour growth, limit the production of cancer-related hormones and generally work as antioxidants.

vi. Isothiocyanates

- ellagic acid
- resveratrol

Plant Source

Cruciferous vegetables (broccoli, cabbage, collard greens, kale, cauliflower and Brussels sprouts).

Possible Benefits

May induce detoxification of carcinogens, block tumour growth and work as antioxidants.

vii. Polyphenols

- ellagic acid
- resveratrol

Plant Source

Green tea, grapes, wine, berries, citrus fruits, apples, whole grains and peanuts.

Possible Benefits

May prevent cancer formation, prevent inflammation and work as antioxidants.

viii. Polyphenols

- perillyl alcohol
- limonene, carnosol

Plant Source

Cherries, citrus fruit peel, rosemary.

Possible Benefits

May protect cells from becoming cancerous, slow cancer cell growth, strengthen immune function, limit production of cancer-related hormones, fight viruses, and work as antioxidants.

II

Health benefits from phytochemicals

Phyto means plants in greek, the substances in plants that may prevent diseases like cancer and heart disease. The bioactive non-nutrient plant compounds in fruit, vegetables, grains, and other plant foods—have been linked to reductions in the risk of major chronic diseases. Carotenoids are a class of more than 600 naturally occurring pigments synthesized by plants, algae, and photosynthetic bacteria. These richly coloured molecules are the sources of the yellow, orange, and red colours of many plants. Fruit and vegetables provide most of the carotenoids in the human diet. Nutraceutical-specific chemical compounds in food, including vitamins and additives, may aid in preventing disease. Lycopene is a bright red carotene and carotenoid pigment and phytochemical found in tomatoes and other red fruits and vegetables, such as red carrots.

1. **Phytochemicals**
2. **Eat colours wheel to become fit**
3. **Carotenoids, lycopene and Anthocyanins**
4. **Antioxidants**
5. **Conclusion**

1. Phytochemicals

There are 3,000 different phytochemicals with possible health benefits were reported

- Phytochemicals are certain organic components of plants which scientists have isolated as being beneficial to human health in a different way from traditional antioxidants.
- They are sometimes referred to as phytonutrients, but unlike the traditional nutrients (protein, fat, vitamins, minerals), they are not "essential" for life so the term phytochemical is more accurate.
- Biologically active chemical compounds are found in plants. They are not nutrients like vitamins or minerals. Believed to have health benefits especially related to heart disease and cancer.
- They may serve as antioxidants in a bodily system when required; for example, the phytochemical beta-carotene can metabolize to create vitamin A, a powerful antioxidant
- Additionally, phytochemicals may enhance immune response and cell-to-cell communication, allowing for the body's built-in defences to work more efficiently.
- Phytochemicals may even alter estrogen metabolism, cause cancer cells to die (apoptosis), repair DNA damage caused by smoking and other toxic exposure, and detoxify carcinogens..

Some of the important food sources

- Soy
- Tomato
- Broccoli
- Garlic
- Flax seeds
- Citrus fruits
- Melons: cantaloupe, watermelon
- Pink grapefruit and Blueberries
- Chilli peppers
- Legumes: beans, and lentils

ॐ

2. Eat colours wheel for better health

The colourful pigments are very important, they contain phytochemicals and vitamins.

1. **Red pigments**: Lycopene, phytoene, phytofluene, vitamin E- e.g, Tomatoes, tomato sauce, vegetable juice, tomato soup, watermelon.
2. **Green pigments:** Glucosinolates, Isothiocyanates, Indole-3 Carbinol, and Folic Acid, e.g, Broccoli, Brussel Sprouts, Bok Choy, Cauliflower, Cabbage
3. **Green/Yellow:** Lutein, Zeaxanthin e.g, Spinach, Avocado, Kale, Green Beans, Green Peppers, Kiwi, Collard Greens, Mustard Greens
4. **Orange pigments:** Alpha and Beta Carotene,e.g, Carrots Pumpkins, Squash, Mangos, Apricots, Cantaloupe
5. **Orange/Yellow:** Vitamin C, Flavonoids e.g, Oranges, Orange Juice, Tangerines, Peaches, Lemons, Limes, Pineapple.
6. **Red-Purple pigments:** Anthocyanins, Ellagic Acid, Flavonoids,e.g, Grapes and grape juice, cherries, red wine, strawberries, raisins.
7. **White/ Green:** Allyl Sulfides, e.g, Garlic, Onion, and Chives.

ॐ

3. Carotenoids, Lycopene and Anthocyanins

Carotenoids

Carotenoids are a class of more than 600 naturally occurring pigments synthesized by plants, algae, and photosynthetic bacteria. These richly coloured molecules are the sources of the yellow, orange, and red colours of many plants Fruit and vegetables provide most of the carotenoids in the human diet. There are several dozen carotenoids in the foods and most of these carotenoids have antioxidant activity. There are over 600 known carotenoids; they are split into two classes, xanthophylls and carotenoids. Probably the most well-known carotenoid is the one that gives this second group its name, carotene, found in carrots and is responsible for their bright orange colour. Crude palm oil, however, is the richest source of carotenoids in nature. Their colour, ranging from pale yellow through bright orange to deep red, is directly linked to their structure. Xanthophylls are often yellow, hence their class name.

Humans and animals are mostly incapable of synthesizing carotenoids and must obtain them through their diet. Carotenoids are also actively concentrated in the corpus luteum of the ovaries, where they impart the characteristic colour and may act as general antioxidants.

Lycopene

Lycopene is the natural substance responsible for the deep red colour in many foods, most particularly in tomatoes. It is familiar with lycopene because of the many health benefits it provides such as a cancer-fighting agent and a powerful antioxidant. Found in red carrots, a type of carotene also found in tomatoes. It is believed to help prevent heart disease and, in conjunction with other phytochemicals, reduce the risk of certain cancers, including prostate cancer. The lycopene content of tomatoes depends on species and increases as the fruit ripens.

Health Benefits

Lycopene is well known specifically to help prevent many forms of cancer as well as the prevention and treatments of many illnesses and diseases such as:

- Heart diseases-Lycopene stops LDL cholesterol from being oxidized by free radicals and in turn, cannot be deposited in the plaques which narrow and hardens the arteries
- Infertility-Research suggests that lycopene may help in the treatment of infertility. Results from tests showed that lycopene can boost sperm concentration in men
- Helps prevent diabetes
- Prevents age-related macular degeneration and cataracts
- Prevents the aging of skin and keeps it younger looking
- Acts as an internal sunscreen and protects your skin from sunburn
- Lycopene is also been known to help prevent osteoporosis.

Anthocyanins

More than 500 different anthocyanins have been described in the literature. Anthocyanins are water-soluble phytochemicals with a typical red to blue colour. Anthocyanins belong to the group of flavonoids They are food bioactive compounds implication for cardiovascular disease risk protection. Anthocyanins and pigments of the flavonoid class are found in purple carrots. They occur in all tissues of higher plants they are clear, white to yellow counterparts of anthocyanins occurring in plants.

They can be found in the tissues of plants, including leaves, stems, roots, flowers and fruits of blackcurrant, blueberry, bilberry, cherry, red grape and purple corn. They occur mainly as glycosides of anthocyanidins such as cyanidin, delphinidin, peonidin, pelargonidin, petunidin and malvidin.

HealthBenefits

Although anthocyanins are powerful antioxidants in vitro, their real biological activity will be low because of their low stability and poor absorption. Most studies on the potential health benefits of anthocyanins have been focused on its effect on cardiovascular health, its anti-cancer activity and anti-inflammatory properties. In the human body, these pigments act as powerful antioxidants, immobilizing harmful free radicals. Anthocyanins can also help to reduce the risk of heart disease by slowing blood clotting.

Cardiovascular health

The beneficial biological effects of anthocyanins on cardiovascular health may be driven by their affinity for proteins and their antioxidant activity. Anthocyanins can act on different cells involved in the development of atherosclerosis.

Anticancer

Studies have shown that anthocyanins may act as anti-cancer agents by inhibiting the promotion and progression of tumour cells by stopping the growth of pre-malignant cells, increasing the apoptosis of cancer cells and inhibiting the growth of new blood vessels that nourish tumours.

Anti-inflammatory

The anti-inflammatory action of anthocyanins may be attributed to its direct and strong antioxidant action but also its regulatory effect on the expression of genes involved in the inflammatory response. They also protect the plant cells against damage caused by UV radiation.

Anthocyanin

Use

Anthocyanins are water-soluble strong colours and have been used to colour food since historical times. Extracts of berries have been used to colour drinks, pastries and other foods.

The colour is also susceptible towards temperature, oxygen, UV-light and different co- factors. Temperature may destroy the flavylium ion, and thus causes loss of colour. Oxygen may destroy the anthocyanins, as do other oxidizing reagents, such as peroxides and vitamin C. Many other components in plants and foods may interact with the anthocyanins and either destroy, change or increase the colour. Quinones in apples, for example, enhance the degradation of anthocyanins

Flavonoids are also commonly considered phenols, although the term "flavonoids" can refer to many phytonutrients. Isoflavones are usually categorized as members of this family. They are found in soy, kudzu, red clover, flax and rye, and have been researched extensively for their ability to protect against hormone-dependent cancers, such as breast cancer

Xanthophylls, similar to beta-carotene, give yellow carrots their golden colours; they are linked to eye health and may reduce the incidence of lung and other cancers.

Geraniol

Geraniol is acyclic monoterpene-alcohol. Pure geraniol is a colourless oily liquid, with a sweet rose-like scent. When oxidized, geraniol becomes geranial or citral. It is present in Bergamot, carrot, coriander, lavender, lemon, lime, nutmeg, orange, rose, blueberry and blackberry

Health benefits

Geraniol is a natural antioxidant and prevent cancer as well as Geraniol inhibits DNA synthesis.

Limonene

Pure limonene is a clear liquid. Limonene is a monoterpene, made up of two isoprene units. Limonene occurs in two optically active forms, l-limonene and d- limonen. Both isomers have different odours: l-limonene smells piney and turpentine like and d-limonene has a pleasing orange scent.

Distribution

Limonene is found in the essential oils of citrus fruits and many other plant species. Industrial limonene is produced by by alkali extraction of citrus residues and steam distillation. This distillate contains more than 90% d-limonene. It is a colourless liquid hydrocarbon classified as a cyclic terpene. The more common d-isomer possesses a strong smell of oranges.

Health benefits

Studies have shown that limonene have anti- cancer effects. It increase the levels of liver enzymes involved in detoxifying carcinogens. The Glutathione S- transferase (GST) is a system which eliminates carcinogens. Limonene seems to promote the GST system in the liver and small bowel, thereby decreasing the damaging effects of carcinogens.

Allicin

Allicin

Allicin is an organosulfur compound obtained from garlic, a species in the family Alliaceae. It was first isolated and studied in the laboratory by Chester J. Cavallito and John Hays Bailey in 1944. Allicin is garlic's defence mechanism against attacks by pests. When the garlic plant is attacked or injured it produces allicin by an enzymatic reaction. Allicin, one of the active principles of freshly crushed garlic homogenates, has a variety of antimicrobial properties.

Health benefits

The main antimicrobial effect of allicin is due to its chemical reaction with thiol groups of enzymes, e.g. alcohol dehydrogenase, thioredoxin reductase, and RNA polymerase. Many clinical studies have showed that garlic/allicin has the ability to lower total cholesterol, LDL, or "bad cholesterol" and triglycerides, and increase HDL cholesterol. This in turn prevention of heart-related conditions such as heart attack, atherosclerosis, and stroke. In addition, garlic/allicin may support the overall health of the circulatory system, which may helps in lowering the risk of heart attack and strokes, anti-blood coagulation, anti-hypertension, anti-cancer, antioxidant and anti-microbial effects.

Silymarin

Silymarin is a unique flavonoid complex—containing silybin, silydianin, and silychrisin. These unique phytochemicals . Silymarin is a antioxidant or free radical scavenger. Skin care products often contain silymarin because it antioxidant activity may reduce the risk for skin cancer risk. It provides protection against different stages of induced carcinogenesis protects the liver by promoting the growth of new liver cells. Silymarin has also anti-atherosclerotic activity, by inhibiting the expression of adhesion molecules.

Lutein

Lutein is one of the hydroxy carotenoids found in yellow and orange carrots and makes up the macular pigment of human retinas. Consuming foods high in lutein may increase the density of this pigment and decrease the risk for developing macular degeneration and other age-related diseases.

Flavonoids are a group of plant metabolites thought to provide health benefits through cell signalling pathways and antioxidant effects. These molecules are found in a variety of fruits and vegetables and include over 6,000 already-identified family members Flavonoids are polyphenolic molecules and are soluble in water.

Many flavonoids act as antioxidants

- May protect against cancers and heart disease by this mechanism
- More evidence is needed before any claims can be made for flavonoids themselves as the protective factor in foods

· Particularly when they are extracted from foods or herbs and sold as supplements

☙

4. Antioxidant

An antioxidant is a molecule that inhibits the oxidation of other molecules. Oxidation is a chemical reaction involving the loss of electrons or an increase in oxidation state. Oxidation reactions can produce free radicals. In turn, these radicals can start chain reactions. Lower blood pressure.

Antioxidants are chemicals that interact with and neutralize free radicals, thus preventing them from causing damage. Antioxidants are also known as "free radical scavengers." The body makes some of the antioxidants it uses to neutralize free radicals. All living organisms utilize oxygen to metabolize and use the dietary nutrients in order to produce energy for survival. Vitamin C is the most important water-soluble antioxidant in extracellular fluids and also regenerating vitamin E.. Vitamin E is the most important lipid soluble antioxidant.

Antioxidants within the human body

The antioxidant enzymes – glutathione peroxidase, catalase, and superoxide dismutase (SOD) are such enzymes. They require micronutrient cofactors such as selenium, iron, copper, zinc, and manganese for their activity. Antioxidants are used as food additives. These preservatives include natural antioxidants such as ascorbic acid (AA, E300) and tocopherols (E306).

Antioxidants are important

- free radicals are molecules missing electrons: unstable
- formation of 1 free radical causes a chain reaction with many free radicals formed
- antioxidants prevent formation of free radicals or break the chain reaction by becoming oxidized
- Black tea may lower LDL cholesterol
- Improved blood flow and blood vessel function
- Memory and Immune function

- ◦ Oral health
- ◦ Decreased risk of kidney stones and Obesity

Phytoestrogens are plant-based compounds that are structurally similar to estrogen, the primary female sex hormone. Although phytoestrogens can perform most of the functions of estrogen, they are generally weaker than the hormone that is produced naturally by the human endocrine system. Phytoestrogens may reduce risk of adult bone loss and the sensation of elevated body temperature known as "hot flashes". A *diet* high in soy may offer bone protection rivaling that of hormone replacement therapy (HRT).

Xanthophylls

Xanthophylls are the typical yellow pigments of leaves. These are oxygenated carotenoids that are synthesized within the plastids.Xanthophyll**s** do not require light for synthesis, so that xanthophylls are present in all young leaves as well as in etiolated leaves. Dietary carotenoids, especially *xanthophylls*, have attracted significant attention because of their characteristic biological activities.

Xanthophylls are present in two large protein-cofactor complexes, present in photosynthetic membranes of organisms using Photosystem I or Photosystem

Food source

Xanthophylls are found in all young leaves and in etiolated leaves. Examples of other rich sources include papaya, peaches, prunes, and squash, which contain lutein diesters An **essential nutrient** is a nutrient required for normal human body function that either cannot be synthesized by the body at all, or cannot be synthesized in amounts adequate for good health (e.g., niacin,choline), and thus must be obtained from a dietary source.

Lycopene is not an essential nutrient for humans, but is commonly found in the diet mainly from dishes prepared from tomatoes. When absorbed from the intestine, lycopene is transported in the blood by various lycoproteins and accumulates primarily in the blood, adipose tissue, skin, liver, and adrenal glands, but can be found in most tissues. Carotenoids like lycopene are important pigments found in photosynthetic. They are responsible for the bright colours of fruits and vegetables, perform various functions in photosynthesis, and protect photosynthetic organisms from excessive light damage. Lycopene in tomato paste is up to four times more bioavailable than in fresh tomatoes. While most green leafy vegetables and other sources of lycopene are low in fats and oils, lycopene is insoluble in water and is tightly bound to vegetable fiber. Processed tomato products such as pasteurized tomato juice, soup, sauce, and ketchup contain the highest concentrations of bioavailable lycopene from tomato-based sources. Lycopene is fat-soluble, so the oil is said to help absorption. Lycopene may be obtained from vegetables and fruits such as the tomato. The cis-lycopene from some varieties of tomato is more bioavailable. An example is the blood orange, which is coloured by anthocyanins, while other red coloured oranges, and other citrus fruit are coloured by lycopene.

Higest activity found in these foods

Highest anticancer activity can be found in garlic, soybeans, cabbage, ginger, licorice root, and the umbelliferous vegetables.

Additional foods found to have cancer protective activity: onions, flax, citrus, turmeric, cruciferous veggies, tomatoes, sweet peppers and brown rice.

- Soybeans and soy products.
- Tempeh.
- Linseed (flax)
- Sesame seeds.
- Wheatberries.
- Fenugreek (contains diosgenin, but also used to make Testofen®, a compound taken by men to increase testosterone).
- Oats.
- Barley.

Phyto means plants in greek, the substances in plants that may prevent diseases like cancer and heart disease. The bioactive non nutrient plant compounds in fruit, vegetables, grains, and other plant foods—have been linked to reductions in the risk of major chronic diseases. Carotenoids are a class of more than 600 naturally occurring pigments synthesized by plants, algae, and photosynthetic bacteria. These richly coloured molecules are the sources of the yellow, orange, and red colours of many plants . Fruit and vegetables provide most of the carotenoids in the human diet. Nutraceutical - specific chemical compounds in food, including vitamins and additives, that may aid in preventing disease. Lycopene is a bright red carotene and carotenoid pigment and phytochemical found in tomatoes and other red fruits and vegetables, such as red carrots.

1. Phytochemicals
2. Eat colours Wheel to become fit
3. Carotenoids , lycopens and Anthocyanins
4. Antioxidents
5. Conclusion:

1. Phytochemicals

There are 3,000 different phytochemicals with possible health benefits were reported

- Phytochemicals are certain organic components of plants which scientists have isolated as being beneficial to human health in a different way from traditional antioxidants.
- They are sometimes referred to as phytonutrients, but unlike the traditional nutrients (protein, fat, vitamins, minerals), they are not "essential" for life so the term phytochemical is more accurate.
- Biologically active chemical compounds found in plants.They are not nutrients like vitamins or minerals.Believed to have health benefits especially related to heart disease and cancer.
- They may serve as antioxidants in a bodily system when required; for example, the phytochemical beta-carotene can metabolize to create vitamin A, a powerful antioxidant
- Additionally, phytochemicals may enhance immune response and cell-to-cell communication, allowing for the body's built-in defenses to work more efficiently.
- Phytochemicals may even alter estrogen metabolism, cause cancer cells to die (apoptosis), repair DNA damage caused by smoking and other toxic exposure, and detoxify carcinogen..

Some of the important food sources

- Soy
- Tomato
- Broccoli
- Garlic
- Flax seeds
- Citrus fruits
- Melons: cantaloupe, watermelon
- Pink grapefruit and Blueberries
- Chili peppers
- Legumes: beans, and lentils

2. Eat colours wheel for better health

The colourful pigments are very important, they contain phytochemicals and vitamins,eg

1. Red pigments : Lycopene, phytoene, phytofluene, vitamin E- eg,Tomatoes, tomato sauce, vegetable juice, tomato soup, watermelon.
2. Green pigments: Glucosinolates, Isothiocyanates, Indole-3 Carbinol, and Folic Acid,eg Broccoli, Brussel Sprouts, Bok Choy, Cauliflower , Cabbage
3. Green/Yellow- Lutein, Zeaxanthin
4. Spinach, Avocado, Kale , Green Beans, Green Peppers, Kiwi, Collard Greens, Mustard Greens
5. Orange pigments : Alpha and Beta Carotene,eg Carrots Pumpkins, Squash, Mangos, Apricots, Cantaloupe
6. Orange/Yellow: Vitamin C, Flavonoids eg,Oranges, Orange Juice, Tangerines, Peaches, lemons, Limes, Pineapple.
7. Red-Purple pigments :Anthocyanins, Ellagic Acid, Flavonoids,eg,Grapes and grape juice, cherries, red wine, strawberries, raisins
8. White/ Green : Allyl Sulfides,eg, Garlic, Onion, and Chives

3. Carotenoids, lycopenes and Anthocyanins

Carotenoids

Carotenoids are a class of more than 600 naturally occurring pigments synthesized by plants, algae, and photosynthetic bacteria. These richly coloured molecules are the sources of the yellow, orange, and red colours of many plants Fruit and vegetables provide most of the carotenoids in the human diet.There are several dozen carotenoids in the foods and most of these carotenoids have antioxidant activity.

There are over 600 known carotenoids; they are split into two classes, xanthphylls and cartonoids.Probably the most well-known carotenoid is the one that gives this second group its name,carotene, found in carrots and are responsible for their bright orange colour. Crude palm oil, however, is the richest source of carotenoids in nature.Their colour, ranging from pale yellow through bright orange to deep red, is directly linked to their structure. Xanthophylls are often yellow, hence their class name.

Humans and animals are mostly incapable of synthesizing carotenoids and must obtain them through their diet. Carotenoids are also actively concentrated in the corpus luteum of the ovaries, where they impart the characteristic colour, and may act as general antioxidants.

Lycopene

Lycopene is the natural substance responsible for the deep red colour in many foods, most particularly in tomatoes. It is familiar with lycopene because of of the many health benefits it provides such as a cancer fighting agent and a powerful antioxidant.

Found in red carrots, is a type of carotene also found in tomatoes. It is believed to help prevent heart disease and, in conjunction with other phytochemicals, reduce the risk of certain cancers, including prostate cancer. The lycopene content of tomatoes depends on species and increases as the fruit ripens.

Health Benefits

Lycopene is well known specifically to help prevent many forms of cancer as well as the prevention and treatments of many illnesses and diseases such as:

- Heart diseases-Lycopene stops LDL cholesterol from being oxidized by free radicals and in turn cannot be deposited in the plaques which narrows and hardens the arteries
- Infertility-Research suggests that lycopene may help in the treatment of infertility. Results from tests showed that lycopene can boost sperm concentration in men
- Helps prevent diabetes
- Prevents age-related macular degeneration and cataracts
- Prevents the aging of skin and keeps it younger looking
- Acts as an internal sunscreen and protects your skin from sunburn
- Lycopene is also been known to help prevent osteoporosis.

Anthocyanins

More than 500 different anthocyanins have been described in the literature. Anthocyanins are water-soluble phytochemicals with a typical red to blue colour. Anthocyanins belong to the group of flavonoids They are food bioactive compounds implication on cardiovascular disease risk protection. Anthocyanins and pigments of the flavonoid class are found in purple carrots. They occur in all tissuse of higher plants they are clear, white to yellow counterparts of anthocyanins occurring in plants.

They can be found in tissues of plants, including leaves, stems, roots, flowers and fruits of blackcurrant, blueberry, bilberry, cherry, red grape and purple corn. They occur mainly as glycosides of anthocyanidins such as cyanidin, delphinidin, peonidin, pelargonidin, petunidin and malvidin.

HealthBenefits

Although anthocyanins are powerful antioxidants in vitro, their real biological activity will be low because of their low stability and poor absorption. Most studies on the potential health benefits of anthocyanins have been focused on its effect on cardiovascular health, its anti-cancer activity and anti-inflammatory properties. In the human body these pigments act as powerful antioxidants, immobilizing harmful free radicals. Anthocyanins can also help to reduce the risk of heart disease by slowing blood clotting.

Cardiovascular health

The beneficial biological effects of anthocyanins on cardiovascular health may be driven by their affinity for proteins and their antioxidant activity. Anthocyanins can act on different cells involved in the development of arthrosclerosis.

Anticancer

Studies have shown that anthocyanins may act as anti-cancer agents by inhibit promotion and progression of tumor cells by stopping the growth of pre-malignant cells, increasing the apoptosis of cancer cells and inhibiting the growth of new blood vessels that nourish tumors.

Anti-inflammatory

The anti-inflammatory action of anthocyanins may be attributed to its direct and strong antioxidant action but also its regulatory effect on the expression of genes involved in the inflammatory response. They are also protect the plant cells against damage caused by UV radiation

Anthocyanin

Use

Anthocyanins are water soluble strong colours and have been used to colour food since historical times. Extracts of berries have been used to colour drinks, pastries and other foods.

The colour is also susceptible towards temperature, oxygen, UV-light and different co- factors. Temperature may destroy the flavylium ion, and thus causes loss of colour. Oxygen may destroy the anthocyanins, as do other oxidizing reagents, such as peroxides and vitamin C. Many other components in plants and foods may interact with the anthocyanins and either destroy, change or increase the colour. Quinones in apples, for example, enhance the degradation of anthocyanins

Flavonoids are also commonly considered phenols, although the term "flavonoids" can refer to many phytonutrients. Isoflavones are usually categorized as members of this family. They are found in soy, kudzu, red clover, flax and rye, and have been researched extensively for their ability to protect against hormone-dependent cancers, such as breast cancer

Xanthophylls, similar to beta-carotene, give yellow carrots their golden colours; they are linked to eye health and may reduce the incidence of lung and other cancers.

Geraniol

Geraniol is acyclic monoterpene-alcohol. Pure geraniol is a colourless oily liquid, with a sweet rose-like scent. When oxidized, geraniol becomes geranial or citral. It is present in Bergamot, carrot, coriander, lavender, lemon, lime, nutmeg, orange, rose, blueberry and blackberry

Health benefits

Geraniol is a natural antioxidant and prevent cancer as well as Geraniol inhibits DNA synthesis.

Limonene

Pure limonene is a clear liquid. Limonene is a monoterpene, made up of two isoprene units. Limonene occurs in two optically active forms, l-limonene and d- limonen. Both isomers have different odours: l-limonene smells piney and turpentine like and d-limonene has a pleasing orange scent.

Distribution

Limonene is found in the essential oils of citrus fruits and many other plant species. Industrial limonene is produced by by alkali extraction of citrus residues and steam distillation. This distillate contains more than 90% d-limonene. It is a colourless liquid hydrocarbon classified as a cyclic terpene. The more common d-isomer possesses a strong smell of oranges.

Health benefits

Studies have shown that limonene have anti- cancer effects. It increase the levels of liver enzymes involved in detoxifying carcinogens. The Glutathione S- transferase (GST) is a system which eliminates carcinogens. Limonene seems to promote the GST system in the liver and small bowel, thereby decreasing the damaging effects of carcinogens.

Allicin

Allicin

Allicin is an organosulfur compound obtained from garlic, a species in the family Alliaceae. It was first isolated and studied in the laboratory by Chester J. Cavallito and John Hays Bailey in 1944. Allicin is garlic's defence mechanism against attacks by pests. When the garlic plant is attacked or injured it produces allicin by an enzymatic reaction. Allicin, one of the active principles of freshly crushed garlic homogenates, has a variety of antimicrobial properties.

Health benefits

The main antimicrobial effect of allicin is due to its chemical reaction with thiol groups of enzymes, e.g. alcohol dehydrogenase, thioredoxin reductase, and RNA polymerase.

Many clinical studies have showed that garlic/allicin has the ability to lower total cholesterol, LDL, or "bad cholesterol" and triglycerides, and increase HDL cholesterol. This in turn prevention of heart-related conditions such as heart attack, atherosclerosis, and stroke. In addition, garlic/allicin may support the overall health of the circulatory system, which may helps in lowering the risk of heart attack and strokes, anti-blood coagulation, anti-hypertension, anti-cancer, antioxidant and anti-microbial effects.

Silymarin

Silymarin is a unique flavonoid complex—containing silybin, silydianin, and silychrisin. These unique phytochemicals . Silymarin is a antioxidant or free radical scavenger. Skin care products often contain silymarin because it antioxidant activity may reduce the risk for skin cancer risk. It provides protection against different stages

of induced carcinogenesis protects the liver by promoting the growth of new liver cells. Silymarin has also anti-atherosclerotic activity, by inhibiting the expression of adhesion molecules.

Lutein

Lutein is one of the hydroxy carotenoids found in yellow and orange carrots and makes up the macular pigment of human retinas. Consuming foods high in lutein may increase the density of this pigment and decrease the risk for developing macular degeneration and other age-related diseases.

Flavonoids are a group of plant metabolites thought to provide health benefits through cell signalling pathways and antioxidant effects. These molecules are found in a variety of fruits and vegetables and include over 6,000 already-identified family members Flavonoids are polyphenolic molecules and are soluble in water.

Many flavonoids act as antioxidants

- May protect against cancers and heart disease by this mechanism
- More evidence is needed before any claims can be made for flavonoids themselves as the protective factor in foods
- Particularly when they are extracted from foods or herbs and sold as supplements

4. Antioxidant

An antioxidant is a molecule that inhibits the oxidation of other molecules. Oxidation is a chemical reaction involving the loss of electrons or an increase in oxidation state. Oxidation reactions can produce free radicals. In turn, these radicals can start chain reactions. Lower blood pressure.

Antioxidants are chemicals that interact with and neutralize free radicals, thus preventing them from causing damage. Antioxidants are also known as "free radical scavengers." The body makes some of the antioxidants it uses to neutralize free radicals. All living organisms utilize oxygen to metabolize and use the dietary nutrients in order to produce energy for survival. Vitamin C is the most important water-soluble antioxidant in extracellular fluids and also regenerating vitamin E.. Vitamin E is the most important lipid soluble antioxidant.

Antioxidants within the human body

The antioxidant enzymes – glutathione peroxidase, catalase, and superoxide dismutase (SOD) are such enzymes. They require micronutrient cofactors such as selenium, iron, copper, zinc, and manganese for their activity. Antioxidants are used as food additives. These preservatives include natural antioxidants such as ascorbic acid (AA, E300) and tocopherols (E306).

Antoxidants are important

- free radicals are molecules missing electrons: unstable
- formation of 1 free radical causes a chain reaction with many free radicals formed
- antioxidants prevent formation of free radicals or break the chain reaction by becoming oxidized
- Black tea may lower LDL cholesterol
- Improved blood flow and blood vessel function
- Memory and Immune function
- Oral health
- Decreased risk of kidney stones and Obesity

Phytoestrogens are plant-based compounds that are structurally similar to estrogen, the primary female sex hormone. Although phytoestrogens can perform most of the functions of estrogen, they are generally weaker than the hormone that is produced naturally by the human endocrine system. Phytoestrogens may reduce risk of adult bone loss and the sensation of elevated body temperature known as "hot flashes".

A *diet* high in soy may offer bone protection rivaling that of hormone replacement therapy (HRT).

Xanthophylls

Xanthophylls are the typical yellow pigments of leaves. These are oxygenated carotenoids that are synthesized within the plastids.Xanthophyll**s** do not require light for synthesis, so that xanthophylls are present in all young leaves as well as in etiolated leaves. Dietary carotenoids, especially *xanthophylls*, have attracted significant attention because of their characteristic biological activities. **Xanthophylls** are present in two large protein-cofactor complexes, present in photosynthetic membranes of organisms using Photosystem I or Photosystem I

Food source

Xanthophylls are found in all young leaves and in etiolated leaves. Examples of other rich sources include papaya, peaches, prunes, and squash, which contain lutein diesters. An **essential nutrient** is a nutrient required for normal human body function that either cannot be synthesized by the body at all, or cannot be synthesized in amounts adequate for good health (e.g., niacin,choline), and thus must be obtained from a dietary source.

Lycopene is not an essential nutrient for humans, but is commonly found in the diet mainly from dishes prepared from tomatoes. When absorbed from the intestine, lycopene is transported in the blood by various lycoproteins and accumulates primarily in the blood, adipose tissue, skin, liver, and adrenal glands, but can be found in most tissues. Carotenoids like lycopene are important pigments found in photosynthetic.

They are responsible for the bright colours of fruits and vegetables, perform various functions in photosynthesis, and protect photosynthetic organisms from excessive light damage. Lycopene in tomato paste is up to four times more bioavailable than in fresh tomatoes. While most green leafy vegetables and other sources of lycopene are low in fats and oils, lycopene is insoluble in water and is tightly bound to vegetable fiber. Processed tomato products such as pasteurized tomato juice, soup, sauce, and ketchup contain the highest concentrations of bioavailable lycopene from tomato-based sources. Lycopene is fat-soluble, so the oil is said to help absorption. Lycopene may be obtained from vegetables and fruits such as the tomato. The cis-lycopene from some varieties of tomato is more bioavailable. An example is the blood orange, which is coloured by anthocyanins, while other red coloured oranges, and other citrus fruit are coloured by lycopene.

Highest activity found in these foods: Highest anticancer activity can be found in garlic, soybeans, cabbage, ginger, licorice root, and the umbelliferous vegetables.

Additional foods found to have cancer protective activity: onions, flax, citrus, turmeric, cruciferous veggies, tomatoes, sweet peppers and brown rice.

- Soybeans and soy products.
- Tempeh.
- Linseed (flax)
- Sesame seeds.
- Wheatberries.
- Fenugreek (contains diosgenin, but also used to make Testofen®, a compound taken by men to increase testosterone).
- Oats.
- Barley.

III

Antioxidants from Phytochemical for health and medicine

Phytochemicals are the chemicals extracted from plants. These chemicals are classified as primary or secondary constituents, depending on their role in plant metabolism. Primary constituents include the common sugars, amino acids, proteins, purines and pyrimidines of nucleic acids, chlorophyll's etc. Secondary constituents are the remain- ing plant chemicals such as alkaloids (derived from ami- no acids), terpenes (a group of lipids) and phenolics (de- rived from carbohydrates) (Walton et al., 1999).Antioxidants are secondary constituents or metabolites found naturally in the body and in plants such as fruits and vegetables. An antioxidant can be defined in simple terms as anything that inhibits or prevents oxidation of a susceptible substrate. Plants produce a very impressive array of antioxidant compounds that includes carote- noids, flavonoids, cinnamic acids, benzoic acids, folic acid, ascorbic acid, tocopherols and tocotrienols to pre- vent oxidation of the susceptible substrate (Hollman, 2001). Common antioxidants include vitamin A, vitamin C, vitamin E, and certain compounds called carotenoids (like lutein and beta-carotene) (Hayek, 2000). These plant-based dietary antioxidants are believed to have an important role in the maintenance of human health be- cause our endogenous antioxidants provide insufficient protection against the constant and unavoidable challen- ge of reactive oxygen species

(ROS; oxidants) (Fridovich, 1998).

Generation of free radicals or reactive oxygen species (ROS) during metabolism and other activities beyond the antioxidant capacity of a biological system gives rise to oxidative stress (Mikulikova and Popes, 2001). Oxidative stress plays a role in heart diseases, malaria, neurodege- nerative diseases, AIDS, cancer and in the aging process (Sian et al., 2003). This concept is supported by in- creasing evidence that oxidative damage plays a role in the development of chronic, age-related degenerative diseases, and that dietary antioxidants oppose this and lower risk of disease (Atoui et al., 2005; Alasalvar et al., 2005) and thus there arises a necessity to extract these antioxidants from the plant matrices. In a recent study (Grigonisa, 2005) different extraction techniques, such as dispersed-solids, percolation, Soxhlet, microwave assist- ed extraction and supercritical fluid extraction have been used to isolate antioxidants from the plants. Supercritical fluid extraction (SFE) is found to be the feasible and sophisticated technology for the extraction of the antioxi- dants (Nguyen et. al. 1994). The methodology of solid phase extraction (SPE) with super critical fluids such as CO_2 is found to yield higher purity antioxidants.

This review discusses the effect of oxidants on human health and their neutralization by antioxidants. Different types of antioxidants, their properties and their extraction processes from plant matrices have been dealt in detail. Recent advances in supercritical extraction of antioxi- dants are presented.

Formation of oxidants

Oxygen, an essential element for life, can also be a rea- son for the destruction of tissue and/or impair its ability to function normally (Kehrer et al., 1993). Oxidants or free radicals or oxygen-free radicals (OFR) or more generally called as reactive oxygen species (ROS) are formed due to various exogenous and endogenous factors. A free radical contains one or more unpaired electrons and is capable of independent existence. The formation of oxy- gen radicals could be the reason for the damaging effects of O_2. A class of enzymes called superoxide dismutases (SODS) is responsible for the catalytic removal of super- oxide free radical, O⁻ (Lee et al., 2001). An average person has around 10,000–20,000 free radicals attacking each body cell every day. In some cases, ROS are pro- duced specifically to serve essential biological functions, whereas in other cases, they are the byproducts of meta- bolic processes (Shigenaga et al., 1994).

Exogenous sources

Exposure to radiation from the environment and man- made sources is the exogenous source for formation of oxidants. Low-wavelength electromagnetic radiation such as gamma rays splits water in the body to generate hy- droxyl radical, OH^-. The highly reactive OH^- thus formed begins to react vigorously with the nearby cells (Halliwell, 1994). Even though OH^- scavengers usually have rate constants more than 10^{10} M^{-1} sec^{-1} for reaction with OH^-, the most endogenous molecules react equally fast. The antioxidant systems that defend against damage by OH^- do so by preventing its formation and by repairing the damage it causes (Timothy et al., 2003).

It has been estimated that 1-3% of the oxygen we brea- the in is used to make O^-. Since humans consume large quantities of O_2, a simple calculation shows that over 2 kg of O^- is made in the human body every year-people with chronic inflammations may make much more (Halliwell et al., 1994). These oxidants damage cellular macromolecu- les, including DNA, protein and lipid (Fraga et al., 1990) and accumulation of such damage may con- tribute to ageing and age related diseases.

Endogenous sources and characteristics of oxygen radicals

Other than the exogenous sources such as exposure to radiation, enzymatically or non-enzymatically mediated electron transfer reactions are the source of free radicals produced in the cells. Electron leakage that occurs from electron transport chains, such as those in the mitochon- dria and endoplasmic reticulum, to molecular oxygen are the major source of free radicals (Fridovich, 1986).

Oxidants are formed in the cells of our body mainly from the following four endogenous sources.

1. Consumption of O_2 by mitochondria during normal aerobic respiration to produce H_2O. Oxidants such as oxygen free radical, H_2O_2 and hydroxyl radical are the by products of this process
2. Destroying of bacteria and virus infected cells by pha- gogytic cells releases nitric oxide, hydrogen peroxide and oxygen free radical.

3. Degradation of fatty acids and other molecules by peroxisomes, the organelles produce hydrogen peroxide as byproduct, which is then degraded by catalase. The nondegraded peroxide gets into other compartments of nearby cell thereby leading to oxidative DNA damage (Ames et al., 1993). When two free radicals a nonradical is produced due to the formation of covalent bond bet- ween their unpaired electrons. But a radical is formed when a free radical reacts with a nonradical and thus can initiate a chain reaction in the body.

4. Oxidants produced during the course of p. 450 degra-dation of natural toxins.

Organisms have developed many defense mechanisms to limit the level of reactive oxidants and the damage inflicted by them (Sang et al., 2002). Despite the cell's anti-oxidant defense system to counteract oxidative damage from free radicals, radical-related damage of DNA and proteins have been proposed to play a key role in the development of age-dependent diseases such as cancer, arteriosclerosis, arthritis, eurodegenerative disorders and others (Ames, 1989). Reactive oxygen species interacts with cellular components including DNA bases and forms damaged bases or strand breaks (Atoui et al., 2005). Oxygen radicals oxidize lipids or proteins generating inte- mediates that react with DNA by forming adducts. There- fore, it is an utmost necessity to take antioxidants exoge- nously due to the changes in the environment for which man made activities such as deforestation, rise in carbon dioxide level in atmosphere etc., are also responsible factors.

Antioxidant and its mechanism

Antioxidants are defined as the substance that when pr- sent in low concentrations compared to those of an oxidi- sable substrate significantly delays or prevents oxidation of that substance (Halliwell and Guteridge, 1989). For the *in vivo* situation the concept of antioxidants includes anti-oxidant enzymes, iron binding and transport proteins and other compounds affecting signal transduction and gene expression (Gutteridge, 1989). In case of foods and beverages, antioxidants are related to the protection of specific oxidation substrates or the formation of specific oxidation.

Synergism, antagonism, co-antioxidants and oxidation retarders are the other useful concepts related to antioxi- dants. Synergism can be defined as the phenomenon in which a number of compounds, when present together in the same system, have a more pronounced effect than if they were alone (Uri, 1961). Antagonism can be defined likewise by substituting "more" with "less", whereas co- antioxidants may be defined by substituting "more" with "same". The compounds that reduce the rate of oxidation without showing a distinct lag phase of oxidation are retarders of oxidation. Antioxidant action is measured as a decrease in over-all rate of oxidation and as the length of the lag phase.

Antioxidants are divided into two classes: preventive antioxidants and chain breaking antioxidants. Preventive antioxidants inhibit oxidation by reducing the rate of chain initiation. In most cases hydroperoxide product, ROOH of the oxidation is the cause for the initiation process. Preventive antioxidants convert the hydroperoxides to molecular products that are not potential sources of free radicals (Burton et al., 1985). Most biological preventive antioxidants are also peroxide decomposers. Certain enzymes such as glutathione peroxidase can reduce H_2O_2 to H_2O and also lipid hyroperoxides to the corres- ponding alcohol as shown in the following equation (1).

[2H]

$$ROOH \ldots\ldots\ldots\ldots\ldots\ldots ROH + H_2O$$

(1) Glutathione peroxides

Commercial chain breaking antioxidants are generally phenols or aromatic amines. They owe their antioxidant activity to their ability to trap peroxyl radicals are as shown in equation (2).

$$O_2^{\cdot} + Antioxidant\ O_2 + Antioxidant + heat$$

(2)

Antioxidants can also be manufactured synthetically. These belong to the class of synthetic antioxidants. The main disadvantage with these antioxidants is their side effect when taken in vivo (Chen et al., 1992). Most of the natural antioxidants are found to have higher antioxidant activity when compared with that of the synthetic ones. Several arguments suggest that the antioxidant compo- nents of fruits and vegetables contribute in the defense effect. Epidemiological studies and intervention trials on prevention of diseases such as cancer and cardiovascu- lar disease in people have shown the positive effects of taking antioxidant supplements (Ames et al., 1993; Enst- rom et al., 1992; Rimm et al., 1993).

Carotenoids, flavonoids, cinnamic acids, benzoic acids, folic acid, ascorbic acid, tocopherols and tocotrienols are some of the antioxidants produced by the plant for their sustenance. Some of the widely known antioxidants are beta-carotene, ascorbic acid and alpha tocopherol (Mc- Call et al., 1999). Beta-carotene is known as a precursor to vitamin A; it is converted to vitamin A in the liver and the mucous membranes of the small intestine. Beta- carotene is found to be safer as it can be ingested in almost unlimited quantities without toxic effect to the body (Dagenais et al., 2000). Ascorbic acid has multi-functional properties. Based on conditions ascorbic acid can act as an antioxidant, pro-oxidant, a metal chelator, a reducing agent or an oxygen scavenger. Ascorbic acid can act as a pro-oxidant in aqueous systems containing metals, by reducing them, which become more active catalysts of oxidation in their lower valence state. In the absence of added metals, ascorbic acid is an effective antioxidant at high concentrations (Katsunari et al., 1999).

Vitamin E is a group of compounds with well known an- tioxidant functions. Among vitamin E compounds, toco- pherol and especially alphtocopherol possesses the str- ongest biological activity. Tocopherol is prevalently found in mammalian tissue (Flohe et al., 2002)). Se is a natu- rally occurring antioxidant that preserves tissue elas-ticity by delaying oxidation of polyunsaturated fatty acids. Se is an essential component of glutathione peroxidase. Se deficiency has been implicated as contributing factor to the development of cardiovascular disease (congestive cardiomyopathy), accelerated atherosclerosis, skeletal muscle myopathy, increased cancer risk, aging, cataract and deranged immune function (Zima et al., 2004). Small molecule dietary antioxidants such as vitamin C (ascor- bate), vitamin E (tocopherol), and cartoneoids have gene- rated particular interest as anticarcinogens and as de- fenses against degenerative diseases (Leo, 1999). The details of these antioxidants are shown in the Table 1 (Heinerman, 1996; Hashimoto et al., 2002; Cao, 1993; Nessa et al., 2004; Somchit, et al., 2003; Burton, et al., 1985; Halkes, et al., 2002; Burkill, 1993; Oomen and Grubben, 1998 and Zipser, et al., 1998).

Widely used antioxidants and their applications

i. *Antioxidant*

- Beta-Carotene C40H56

Plant sources

- *Elaeis oleifera, Elaeis Guineensis Momordica Cochinchinnensis Spreng Eurycoma Longifolia Zanthoxylum Myriacanthum.*

Applications

Reported to be anodyne, antidotal, aphrodisiac, diuretic, and vulnerary. Oil palm is a folk remedy for headaches, rheumatism and is used as a liniment for indolent tumors. Used as a coloring and flavoring agent in steamed glutinous rice, male aphrodisiac, stomach ache and antitumor agent.

ii. *Antioxidant*

- Alpha-Tocopherol C29H50O2

Plant sources

- *Citrus Hystrix, Calamus Scipronum, Averrhoa Belimbi.*

Applications

Fruit used as preservative, flavoring in both savory and sweet food. Leaves used as hair shampoo and as medicine. The buds of these canes are eaten as food and have medical and antiseptic properties. They are commonly used for treatment of fever and aches. The syrup of the fruit is useful in relieving thirst, febrile excitement, and also in some slight cases of hemorrhage from the bowels, stomach and internal hemorrhoids.

iii. Antioxidant

• Ascorbic Acid C6H8O6

Plant sources

• *Apium Graveolens, Sauropus, Androgynous*

Applications

Arthritis, Back Pain (lower), Nervousness, Rheumatism. Insect and disease resistance.

iv. Antioxidant

• Palmitic Acid CH3(CH2)14COOH

Plant sources

• *Elaeis Oleifera, Guineensis*

Applications

Anodyne, antidotal, aphrodisiac, diuretic and vulnerary. Oil palm is source of palmitic acid and is a folk remedy for cancer, headaches, and rheumatism.

v. Antioxidant

- Beta Sitosterol C29H50O

Plant sources

- *Morinda Citrifolia, Alpinia Officinarum, Sida Acuta*

Applications

Diabetes, high blood pressure, arthritis, skin afflictions, and conditions of aging. Flatulence, dyspepsia, vomiting and sickness at stomach, and recommended as a remedy for stomach cancer. Entire plant for stomach ache.

vi. Antioxidant

- Selenium

Plant sources

- *Astragalus, Membranaceus, Valeriana Officinalis, Achillea Millefolium*

Applications

Prevents severe side effects of chemotherapy in patients with cancer. Inhibits the growth of murine renal cell carcinoma. Activation of immune system. Sedative activity. General tonic for the cardio-vascular system, lowers blood pressure, and slows heartbeat.

vii. Antioxidant

- Selenium

Plant sources

- *Astragalus, Membranaceus, Valeriana Officinalis, Achillea Millefolium*

Applications

Prevents severe side effects of chemotherapy in patients with cancer. Inhibits the growth of murine renal cell carcinoma. Activation of immune system. Sedative activity. General tonic for the cardio-vascular system, lowers blood pressure, and slows heartbeat.

viii. Antioxidant

- Anthraquinone $C_{14}H_8O_2$

Plant sources

- *Cassia Acutifolia*

Applications

Antihelminthic, antibacterial, laxative, diuretic, for treatment of snakebites and uterine disorders.

ix. Antioxidant

- Tannic acid C76H52O46

Plant sources

- *Costus Spinosa*

Applications

Tanning of leather

xi. Antioxidant

- Quercetin C15H10O7

Plant sources

- *Blumea Balsamifera*

Applications

Treatment for the swelling of pancreas

Antioxidant and cancer

It has been estimated that one human cell is exposed to approximately 105 oxidative hits a day from hydroxyl radical and other such species of oxidants. ROS are normal oxidant by-products of aerobic metabolism, and under normal metabolic conditions about 2–5% of O_2 consumed by mitochondria is converted to ROS (Lopaczynsk and Zeisel, 2001 and Dreher et al., 1996). Oxidative stress thus created permanently modifies the genetic material leading to numerous degenerative or chronic diseases, such as atherosclerosis and cancer (Ames et al., 1993). Misrepair of DNA damage could result in mutations such as base substitution and deletion which could lead to carcinogenesis (Barcellos, 2005). Two different mecha- nisms are thought to play a role in oxidative damage and in the development of carcinogenesis.

The first mechanism is through the modulation of gene expression. Epigenetic effects on gene expression can lead to the stimulation of growth signals and proliferation (Crawford et al., 1995). Chromosomal rearrangements are thought to result from strand breakage misrepair, contributing to genetic amplifications, iterations in gene expression and loss of heterozygosity, which in turn may promote neoplastic progression (Bohr et al., 1995). Active oxygen species have been demonstrated to stimulate protein kinase and poly (ADP ribosylation) pathways, thus affecting signal transduction pathways. This further can lead to modulation of the expression of essential genes for proliferation and tumour promotion (Cerutti and Trump, 1991). There is a suggestion that free radical sig- nal may be mediated through *ras* signal transduction pathways (Lander et al., 1995).

In the second mechanism, radicals induce genetic alte- rations, such as mutations and chromosomal rearran- gements, which can play a role in the initiation of carcino- genesis (Guyton and Kensler, 1993; Cerda and Weitz- man, 1997). Oxidative DNA damage results in a wide range of chromosomal abnormalities, causing a blockage of DNA replication and wide cytotoxicity (Bohr et al., 1995). Mutations can occur through misrepair or due to incorrect replication, while chromosomal rear-rangements can result from strand breakage misrepair.

It is known that repair mechanisms decay with age and thus DNA lesions accumulate with age (Jaruga and Diz- daroglu, 1996). The sequence specificity of DNA da- mage sites affects the mutation frequency (Dizdaroglu et al., 2002). Therefore, investigation of the sequence speci- ficity of DNA damage would be beneficial for cancer prevention. Mutagenic potential is directly proportional to the number of oxidative DNA lesions that escape repair.

Antioxidant extraction processes

Plants contain a wide spectrum of metabolites, as many as 200,000 different compounds (Fiehn, 2002), although not every metabolite occurs in every species. These me- tabolites represent many different classes of compounds and their derivatives such as amino acids, fatty acids, carbohydrates, and organic acids. The physical-chemical properties of the metabolites are highly variable. There- fore appropriate extraction protocols have to be chosen, as the optimum extraction conditions differ widely for different types of compounds. The plant tissue must be homogenized properly in order to extract plant metaboli- tes efficiently. Various techniques such as grind-ing with a mortar and pestle together with liquid nitrogen, milling in vibration mills with chilled holders, homogeni-zation with a metal pestle connected to an electric drill (Edlund et al., 1995) and ultra-turrax devices (Orth et al., 1999) are available. The degree of homogenization deter-mines the efficiency at which the solvent can penetrate the tis- sue, and therefore strongly influences the length of time required for solvent extraction. The most common way to extract metabolites is to shake the homogenized plant tissue at low or high temperatures in organic sol-vents, or mixtures of solvents (Fiehn et al., 2000). Methanol, etha- nol, and water are the solvents mostly used for extracting polar metabolites, whereas chloroform is the most com- mon solvent for non-polar ones. Alternative extraction techniques include subcritical water extraction (SWE) (Ozel, 2003), pressurized liquid extraction (PLE) (Rostag- no et al., 2004), microwave-assisted extraction (MAE) (Shu et al., 2003) and supercritical fluid extraction (SFE) (Roger, 1999)

Different extraction techniques, such as Soxhlet, micro- wave assisted extraction (MAE) and supercritical fluid extractions (SFE) (Lopez-sebastian et al., 1998) have been used to isolate antioxidants from the plants. Each extraction has its own advantages and disadvantages. The main disadvantages of Soxhlet extraction are long extraction time, degradation of thermolabile compounds and limited solvent choice (Lao et al., 1996). Other con- ventional liquid–solid extraction procedures also are time- consuming, require large amounts of solvents that some- times are hazardous compounds, and consequently require further clean-up and concentration steps. Recent- ly MAE (Eskilson and Bjorklund, 2000) has been used as an alternative laboratory scale extraction method, which proved to be considerably faster. MAE also requires less solvent and provides higher recoveries compared to Soxhlet extraction. The major disadvantage with MAE is that it is usually performed at higher temperatures (110– 150 ∘C).

This temperature range may lead to the denatu- ration of the thermo labile compounds (Kaufmann and Christen, 2002).

Supercritical fluid extraction (SFE) with carbondioxide as supercritical fluid is a very attractive method for extrac- tion (Guarise et al., 1994). This is because CO_2 is inert, non-flammable, non-explosive, inexpensive, odorless, co- lorless, clean solvent that leaves no solvent residue in the product. Moreover, the critical temperature of carbon dioxide being 304° K makes it attractive for the extraction of thermo labile compounds (Tonthubthimthong et al., 2001). However, carbon dioxide is restricted by its inade- quate solvating power for highly polar analytes, which can, to some extent, be boosted by using an appropriate modifier (Zima et al., 2004). SFE modifiers such as etha- nol are introduced at the levels of 1–10%; large modifier concentrations (10 – 50%) are also of interest in some applications. Optimization of the operating conditions such as pressure, percentage of modifier, the fluid pres- sure and temperature and the extraction time are gene- rally considered as the most important factors for good recoveries (Goli et al., 2005).

The results of comparison of different extraction proce- dures for isolation of the antioxidant 5,8 dihydroxycouma- rin from sweet grass (*Hierochlo''e odorata*) were done by Grigonisa, et al., 2005. High yield of 0.58% and concen- tration of 40.4% were obtained for Soxhlet extraction. But this method of extraction is not always acceptable for Industrial applications due to long extraction time, large consumption of hazardous solvents. SFE extraction could be an alternative, as giving second best compound yield of 0.46% and a concentration of 20.3%. MAE was less successful because of lower 5, 8 dihydroxycoumarin ext- raction yield of 0.30%. When comparing extraction time it can be noted that MAE requires 15 min where-as SFE requires 1 to 2 h. However the former requires some time for extract to cool down; consequently total MAE and extract cooling time becomes longer. Soxhlet and micro- wave assisted extraction are unsuitable for thermolabile antioxidants. The major disadvantage of high modifier consumption in SFE can be significantly reduced by recycling. Therefore, SFE can be recommended as a sui- table method to isolate antioxidants.

For medicinal plants the use of sampling techniques such as Soxhlet extraction, microwave assisted extrac- tion (MAE), or pressurized liquid extraction (PLE) often results in non-selective extraction of relatively large amo- unts of undesirable components (e.g. lipids, sterols, chlo- rophylls), which can severely affect the quality of the product (Huie, 2002). Direct supercritical fluid extraction process, in which the chemicals are extracted directly from the plant matrices by the action of supercritical carbondioxide (Catchpole et al., 2002) is also in most cases is subjected to the additional clean-up procedures before the extract is made into useful product. Solid phase ext- raction is a popular and effective tool not only for the clean up, but also for the extraction and/or concentration of analytes.

Solid-phase extraction (SPE) is a simple preparation technique based on the principles used in liquid chroma- tography, in which the solubility and functional group inte- ractions of sample, solvent, and adsorbent are optimized to affect the retention and elution (Sargenti and McNair, 1998). Moderately polar to polar analytes are extracted from non-polar solutions onto polar sorbents. Sorbents for normal phase are modified with cyano- , diol- or amino groups. Non-polar to-moderately polar analytes are extracted from polar solutions onto non-polar sorbents (Tekel and Hatrik, 1996). Chemically modified adsorbent materials such as silica gel and synthetic resins enable precise group separation on the basis of different types of physicochemical interaction. Methods combining solid phase extraction with supercritical fluid technology name- ly indirect supercritical fluid extraction (Khundker et al., 1995) have been employed to extract phytochemicals from aqueous matrices and are found to result in higher yield, concentration and purity of the antioxidant.

IV

Phytochemicals from soy plant and nutritional health benefits

Soy protein has increased attention in recent years among consumers, and researchers. Botanically, soybean belongs to the order Rosaceae, family Leguminosae, the genus Glycine and the cultivar Glycine max. A recent study found that individuals with a habitually health-conscious lifestyle were more likely to consume soy foods than the average person.[1] The purpose of this article is to review the uses and benefits of soy protein foods in normal as well as during pregnancy, postpartum, or infancy. Soybean is a legume that contains no cholesterol and is low in saturated fat.[2] Soybeans are the only vegetable food that contains all eight essential amino acids.[3] Soybeans are also a good source of fiber, iron, calcium, zinc, and B vitamins [Tables 1, 2 and 3].[2] This column reviews the health benefits of soy products with a special focus on human's health including menopausal symptoms, and cancer.[4]

Benefits of soy protein

Soy protein is a high-quality plant-based protein that is equal in protein quality to meat, milk, and eggs. In fact, soy protein is a measure of the digestibility and availability of essential amino acids. Soy protein is very beneficial in various disorders and diseases.[5]

Heart disease

Cardiovascular disease is one of the major health problems in most developed countries. Most deaths due to cardiovascular disease (CVD) are preventable through a lifestyle based on diet, exercise, and no smoking.[6] Soy protein consumption may help lower total blood cholesterol and LDL-cholesterol compared to animal protein consumption.[7] LDL ("bad") cholesterol plays a key role in increasing the risk of coronary heart disease. In addition, soy protein may have an impact in raising HDL ("good") cholesterol. In addition, the consumption of soy protein or isoflavones is a heart-healthy diet for those with elevated total and LDL cholesterol. Oxidized LDL-cholesterol causes damage to arteries. However, preliminary research suggests that the isoflavone genistein, a main component of soy protein, inhibits the oxidation of LDL-cholesterol leading to improved health.[5] The phytoestrogens (plant compounds that have hormone- like effects; isoflavones are the phytoestrogens found in soy) bind to estrogen receptors and produce similar effects including lowering LDL-cholesterol and increasing high-density lipoproteins.[3] Individuals with elevated cholesterol seem to receive the greatest benefit by consuming soy protein.[8] Individuals need to consume about 25 g of soy protein or more each day to obtain results.[9] The Food and Drug Administration approved the health claim for the relationship between soy product consumption and reduced risk of coronary heart disease.[8] A recent study reveals that soy isoflavones significantly reduced serum total and LDL cholesterol but did not change HDL cholesterol and triacylglycerol. Soy protein that contained enriched or depleted isoflavones also significantly improved lipid profiles.[10]

Blood coagulation

Blood clots are often responsible for completely blocking an artery already narrowed by atherosclerosis. Studies suggest that soy isoflavones, especially genistein, have an opposing effect on blood clot formation. Genistein a nonclassical estrogen receptor modulator could affect platelet aggregation through their direct effect on vascular tissue by regulating the synthesis of vasoactive compounds. This reduction of *platelet* aggregation is mediated through nitric oxide release from vascular tissue.[11]

Blood pressure

Uncontrolled high blood pressure can lead to stroke, heart attack, heart failure or kidney failure. Consumption of soy protein may be linked to lower blood pressure. Researchers continue to examine soy protein's effect on blood pressure. In contrast, many soy products should be beneficial to cardiovascular and overall health because of their high content of polyunsaturated fats, fiber, vitamins, and minerals and low content of saturated fat. The effects of soy protein and isoflavones on several other CVD risk factors-HDL cholesterol, triglycerides, lipoprotein (a), and blood pressure-are as follows. Soy protein, like any other dietary protein, contains calories and could be used in the diet to replace animal or vegetable proteins. Soy protein also could replace other sources of calories such as carbohydrate or fat, raising the total amount of protein eaten and reducing carbohydrate or fat intake. Much less is known about the potential impact on risk factors for CVD of increasing total protein intake by adding soy or other plant protein in place of carbohydrate or fat; this important dietary change is currently being studied. A recent result from this randomized, controlled trial indicates that both soy and milk protein intake reduce systolic blood pressure compared with a high-glycemic-index refined carbohydrate among patients with prehypertension and stage-I hypertension. Furthermore, these findings suggest that partially replacing carbohydrate with soy or milk protein might be an important component of nutrition intervention strategies for the prevention and treatment of hypertension.[12]

Cancer

The several bioactive compounds contained in soybeans, such as isoflavones, may help reduce the risk of certain cancers. Genistein, one of the phytochemicals found in soy, can reduce the risk of cancers such as breast cancer, prostate cancer.[9,13] It has been proposed that genistein can prevent tumors and some other kind of cancer by multiple mechanisms. Genistein blocks cancer development by preventing tumors from creating blood vessels that would provide nourishment for growth.[7,9] Soybean foods may be a factor contributing to the diminution of prostate cancer mortality.[14] Genistein has been shown to reduce DNA synthesis in human prostate cells *in vitro* and inhibit testosterone effect in prostate cancer development in rats.[15,16] Another study revealed that soy isoflavone genistein can contribute its anticancer activity for its antioxidant properties. The anticancer effects are more likely due to the fact that genistein is a specific inhibitor of protein tyrosine kinase, MAP kinase, ribosomal S6 kinase, topoisomerase II, which form part of growth factor-stimulated signal transduction cascades in normal and transformed cancer cells. It has also been proved, *in vitro*, that genistein increases concentrations of TGF-β, which may inhibit the growth of cancer cells. Moreover, genistein has an important role as a potent inhibitor of angiogenesis *in vitro*.[17] However, a daily intake of soybean enough to decrease LDL-cholesterol, does not reduce serum prostate specific antigen (PSA) as it has been proposed by others studies.[14] There is some epidemiological evidence for protective effects of soybean products on colon cancer but also a number of studies have shown no effect. *In vitro* studies, soybean products have shown an antiproliferative effect on a wide range of cell types including cells of the gastrointestinal tract.[18] An important role in colon cancer is attributed to dietary fiber, and it also reduces the risk of other chronic diseases in the digestive system.[19,20] Dietary fiber can increase the volume of fecal material and reduce the colonic transit time; therefore it prevents a low fecal material and infrequent bowel movements that can produce a prolonged exposition of colonic cells to fecal mutagens. Moreover, fiber may dilute bile acids and provide a dispersed solid phase in which bile salts can be absorbed reducing their concentration in fecal water, because it has been presumed that bile acid salts may cause chronic irritation in the colon and stimulate colonic mucosal proliferation and therefore act as tumor promoters.[20,21] The fermentation of fiber in colon produces an increase of short-chain fatty acids that present a potential protective effect against colon cancer and bowel infections through inhibition of putrefactive and pathogenic bacteria, respectively.[22,23] Among the short-chain fatty acids, butyrate may act as a regulator of the gene expression that is implicated in colon cells proliferation and differentiation, so it has been proposed that butyrate can be a protection against colon cancer.[18] Dietary flavonoids have shown antiproliferative role for human colon cancer cells. The antiproliferative property of flavonoids could be linked to their ability to inhibit cellular accumulation of ascorbic acid, which is used during cell division. However, there are results showing that isoflavones do not protect against the development of colon cancer in rats treated with a carcinogen and fed with a high fat diet.[18]

Published data about soybean isoflavones and colon cancer are conflicting and scientific evidence in support of the protective effect on colon cancer is limited.[14]

Breast cancer

The growth of both estrogen-dependent and estrogen independent breast cancer cells *in vitro* has been inhibited by genistein, but it is not clear if the concentrations reached *in vitro* could be reached in vivo. The only statement which can be done is that soybean intake may help to prevent the initiation of cancer cells.[19] However, although the hypothesis estrogenic-antiestrogenic effects of isoflavones exits, there is evidence of isoflavones increasing estrogenic activity in risk breast cancer women and in women suffering already breast cancer.[18,24]

Women's health

Diet rich in soy protein has a number of health benefits that are unique to women's needs. A diet rich in soy protein may alleviate certain symptoms associated with menopause, help reduce the risk of breast cancer, promote heart health, and maintain bone health. Soybeans are the only vegetable food that contains all eight essential amino acids.[2,25] Soybeans are also a good source of fiber, iron, calcium, zinc, and B vitamins.[3]

Pregnancy

Use of soy products during pregnancy can be encouraged because expectant women are likely to receive the same health benefits as other women. Fortified milk and fortified soymilk are the only reliable dietary sources of vitamin D.[26] All other dairy products contain little or no vitamin D. While many women will obtain enough vitamin D from exposure to sunlight, soymilk may be an alternative for those who are overly sensitive to the sun or for those who simply are not able to be or do not enjoy being outdoors.

Menopausal symptoms

Phytoestrogens are acting like synthetic estrogen to protect women from bone loss and maintain a healthy heart.[9] Soy protein has been found to positively influence bone and calcium balance in postmenopausal women, especially significant for women not receiving hormone replacement therapy.[27] These results were not seen in young, healthy women who were still menstruating.[28]

Obesity and diabetes

Soy protein control hyperglycemia and reduced body weight, hyperlipidemia, and hyperinsulinemia.[27] These characteristics may be useful to both nondiabetic and diabetic persons in the control of obesity and blood sugar. Soybean therapy in diabetic individuals depends on the type of diabetes and other factors such as lifestyle and metabolic needs of the patients. Soybean protein has a role in diabetes because of its content in glycine and arginine, which tend to reduce blood insulin levels. A soybean fiber may be useful because of its insulin-moderated effect. Soybean diet may be a good option in type 2 diabetes individuals due to its effect on hypertension, hypercholesterolemia, atherosclerosis, and obesity, which are very common diseases in diabetic patients.[29] In addition, substituting animal protein for soybean or other vegetable protein may also decrease renal hyperfiltration, proteinuria, and renal acid load and therefore reduces the risk of renal disease in type 2 diabetes.[30] It is generally accepted that a high fiber diet, particularly soluble fiber, is useful to control plasma glucose concentration in diabetics. In short- and long-term experiments improvement in blood glucose attributed to fiber intake from soybeans has been reported.[21,31] The mechanisms to improve glycemic control during dietary fiber intake seem to be due to the effects of slowing carbohydrate absorption, so that dietary fiber reduces or delays the absorption of carbohydrates.[20] It also increases fecal excretion of bile acid and therefore may cause a low absorption of fat.[30,31] One of the most common complications of diabetes mellitus is the development of diabetic retinopathy. The antiangiogenic effects of isoflavones could be of value in this disorder, although the role of soybean protein isolates containing isoflavones has not been studied in detail.[32] In addition, soybean is associated with health benefits for patients with gallstones. The mechanism of beneficial effect of soybean on gallstones is not well known but it may be related to the blood cholesterol lowering effects of soybean protein containing isoflavones.[29] Researches performed in diabetic patients with soybean diets show several potential advantages, but at the moment very much work is required to define the exact role of soybean in the control of diabetes mellitus.[33]

Nutritional effects

Soy protein can be used as a source of high-quality protein to help satisfy the higher need for protein during muscle-building by providing the necessary essential amino acids for physical and muscular development. While exercise is healthy, it does create oxidant stress that can contribute to muscle soreness, inflammation, and the development of free radicals. It may speed up muscle recovery after exercise. The isoflavones found in soy protein produce antioxidant effects, which may help reduce soreness and inflammation and may help athletes return to the gym more quickly.[34]

Benefits of soy for special populations Vegetarians and vegans

Vegetarians (individuals who do not eat meat) and vegans (individuals who do not eat any products from animals, including eggs, milk, and cheese). Vitamin B12 is only found in animal products and, therefore, may be lacking in the diet of vegans. Use of soymilk is one way to obtain this essential vitamin.[2]

Infants with special conditions

Infants born with lactase deficiency or galactosemia are benefit from the use of soy-based formulas.[2]A vegetarian diet may choose to use a soy-based formula for newborns. In addition, infants who are recovering from episodes of diarrhea (given breast- milk substitutes) may have soy formula recommended to facilitate their recovery. While soy-based formulas meet an infant's growth and development needs, they do not offer any advantage over milk-based formulas.[13] Infants who are not able to tolerate lactose formulas (those based on cow's milk, casein/whey- based formulas; e.g., Similac, Enfamil, Carnation) may be prescribed soy-based formulas if they are not breastfed.[9] Each year, about 20-25% of infants are converted to soy protein formulas (American Dietetic Association and Dieticians of Canada [ADA], 2000). The development of lactose-free cow's milk protein- based formulas has made it unnecessary to switch infants to soy-based formula

(ADA, 2000), though the practice is still common. The use of soy-based formula is effective in only about 20-50% of infants because the soy protein eventually triggers a reaction in susceptible infants.[9]The area of soy protein research has increased in popularity in recent years among multiple health disciplines. Future research efforts are likely to include more scientific advances in the use of soy in the diet. In October 26th, 1999, the Food and Drug Administration (FDA) in USA approved a health claim based on the role of soybean protein in reducing the risk of coronary heart disease.[35] This claim establishes that the soybean protein included in a diet low in saturated fat and cholesterol may reduce the risk of coronary heart disease. The available researches showed that a frequent soybean protein consumption lowers the cholesterol levels.[36,37] The results from recent researches suggest that soybean dietary fiber plays a role in the reduction of cholesterol levels in some hyperlipidemic individuals and has a major protective effect on cardiovascular disease.[38,39] Moreover, it improves the glucose tolerance in some diabetic patients; it increases the wet fecal weight and reduces the caloric density in some foods.[31,40] Dietary fiber seems also to have a positive effect on diarrhea and constipation and as a therapy of irritable bowel syndrome; it has anti-inflammatory and anti-carcinogenic effects on digestive system.[41-43]

Table 1: Nutrition profile of soybeans expressed per 100 g dry matter Composition/Amounts

Complex carbohydrates/(g) 21
Simple carbohydrate/(g) 9
Stachyose/(mg)3,300
Raffinose/(mg)1,600
Protein/(g)36
Total fat/(g)19
Saturated fat/(g)2.8
Monounsaturated fat/(g)4.4
Polyunsaturated fat/(g)11.2
Insoluble fiber/(g)10
Soluble fiber/(g)7
Calcium/(mg)276
Magnesium/(mg)280
Potassium/(mg)1,797
Iron/(mg)16
Zinc/(mg)4.8

Table 2: Amino acid composition of soybean seed[40]
Amino acid/ mg/g protein
Arginine/77.16
Alanine/40.23
Aspartic acid/68.86
Cystine/25.00
Glutamic acid/190.16
Glycine/36.72
Histidine/34.38
4-Hydroxiproline/1.40
Isoleucine/51.58
Leucine/81.69
Lysine/68.37
Methionine/10.70
Phenylalanine/56.29
Proline/52.91
Serine/54.05
Threonine/41.94
Tryptophan/12.73
Tyrosine/41.55
Valine/41.55

V

Phytochemicals with medicinal importance

In recent years, herbal prescriptions have received considerable attention as an alternative way to compensate for perceived deficiencies in orthodox pharmacotherapy worldwide [1]. Despite a lack of medical evidence to support their therapeutic efficacy and toxicological effects, the use of herbal medicine has increased considerably [1]. According to World Health Organization (WHO), up to 80% of the world's population in underdeveloped and developing countries relies on traditional medicine practices for their primary health care needs [2]. Traditional medicines have been accorded greater acceptance in Africa because of the unavailability, unwanted side effects and high costs associated with orthodox medicines, inadequate health facilities and healthcare professionals, coupled with inadequate training of health workers [3]. The therapeutic effects of these medicinal plants can justifiably be attributed to, among others, the phytochemicals in them especially the flavonoids, alkaloids, sterols, terpenoids, phenolic acids, stilbenes, lignans, tannins and saponins.

Phytochemicals are biologically active, naturally occurring chemical compounds found in plants, which protect plant cells from environmental hazards such as pollution, stress, drought, UV exposure and pathogenic attack [4]. These compounds are known as secondary plant metabolites and provide health benefits to humans. They are thought to act as synergistic agents, allowing nutrients to be used more efficiently by the body. Some of the beneficial roles of phytochemicals are low toxicity, low cost, easy availability and their biological properties such as antioxidant activities, antimicrobial effects, modulation of detoxification enzymes, stimulation of the immune system, decrease of platelet aggregation and modulation of hormone metabolism and antineoplastic properties [5].Phytochemicals are not essential nutrients and are not required by the human body for sustaining life, but have important properties to prevent or to fight some common diseases [6]. Because of this property; many studies have been undertaken to

reveal the health benefits of phytochemicals. In this review, we provide an overview of the role of phytochemical compounds present in medicinal herbs in relation to disease management and human health.

Phenolic Compounds

Phenolic compounds are phytochemicals that have one or more aromatic rings with at least one hydroxyl group. In plants, they play a protective role by minimizing the effect of aggression by predators, parasites and also protect plants from ultraviolet radiation. Phenolics and tepernoids are ubiquitous in fruits, cereals, legumes and vegetables. Plant phenolics include flavonoids, phenolic acids, stilbenes, lignans and tannins [7].

1. Flavonoids

Flavonoids are low molecular weight polyphenolic antioxidants naturally present in fruits, vegetables, and beverages such wine and astea [8]. Flavonoids are believed to have various therapeutic values. Flavonoids have been reported to have antihyperglycemic effect [9]. Genistein **(Figure 1)**, an isoflavone is combined with cisplatin, a cytostatic drug to induce apoptosis of BxPC-3 pancreatic carcinoma cells and also reduce proliferation [10]. Nuclear factor kB activation and overexpression reduces the efficacy of chemotherapeutics through inhibition of apoptosis [11]. Genistein down-regulates NF-kB and causes a decrease in expression of anti-apoptotic proteins BclXl and Bcl-2 in xenografts of pancreatic carcinoma cells [12,13]. Genistein and 5-fluoroucil act synergistically to induce p21, Bax and p53 expression in colon cancer HT-29 cells [14]. Genistein and arsenic trioxide combination activates caspase-3 and increases cytochrome-c release thus increases apoptosis in human leukemia cells [15]. These two compounds also work synergistically to stimulate apoptosis and reduce cell viability of hepatocellular carcinoma cell lines [16]. Genistein suppresses glucose uptake in hormone-dependent and hormone-independent breast cancer lines and induces overexpression of glucose-regulated protein 78 involved in cell viability [17-19]. A combination of cisplatin and quercetin have a pro-apoptotic effect on human leukemia and laryngeal carcinoma cells [20]. Cyanidin-o-galactoside, cyanidin-3-o-rutinoside, procyanidin B5and robinetinidol-(4-α-8) catechin-(6,4-α) robinetinol are members of the flavonoid group and their derivatives and are believed to inhibit cell proliferation and have free radical scavenging activity [8].

Flavonoids are known to improve cardiac function, decrease anginas and lowers cholesterol levels. These compounds act by regulation of inflammation mediators [21]. Flavonoids have also been shown to reduce production of pathogenic thrombosis in mice models [22]. A supplement of sea buckthorn which contains high amounts of flavonoids has been shown to restore cardiac function and improve blood circulation in patients with coronary heart disease. Flavonoids have been used in the treatment of chronic cardiac insufficiency and hypertension as they block the activation of necrosis factor kappa-B [23]. Flavonoids like flavone C-glycosid, kakoneinand caesalpin P improves the function of pancreatic islet cells and have diabetic activity [24]. Quercetin has been shown to induce apoptosis in mouse pre-adipocytes and to inhibit adipogenesis [25]. The polyhydroxylated flavonol, myricetin, enhances lipogenesis and glucose uptake in the adipocytes and flavanoid, myricetin has demonstrated insulinomimetic properties [26]. This compound, however, has no effect on insulin receptor auto- phosphorylation. Epicatechinand its active principles have demonstrated that they facilitate insulin release *in vitro* through conversion of pro-insulin to insulin [27]. It has been shown that the flavonoid and flavonoid glycosides cause pancreatic beta cell regranulation and have been used in clinical treatment of diabetes due to improved sensitivity of insulin [28].

Anthocyanins are known to inhibit formation of free radicals thus protecting cardiomyocytes after ischemic episodes [29]. Anthocyanins have vasolidating and antiaggregative activities and also lower levels of oxidized LDL [30]. These compounds are also reported to lower the level of nitric oxide by inhibiting the activity of nitric oxide synthase [31]. Anthocyanins have anti-inflammatory activity as they inhibit cyclooxygenase enzyme. These flavonoids inhibit the expression of VCAM molecules thus inhibiting reaction and adhesion of endothelial cells with leucocytes. These compounds are also believed to decrease the levels of interferon necrosis factor-gamma, interleukin-2 and tumor necrosis factor-alpha and inhibition of mast cell degranulation [32,33]. Proanthocyanins and anthocyanins have antibacterial properties and inhibit adhesion of bacteria to the mucous membrane of the urinary tract [34].

Studies have shown that anthocyanins have protective activity towards paracetamol-induced hepatotoxicity and hepatocytes of hepatitis A and B patients [35,36]. They lower prostaglandin levels by inhibiting COX-2 thus act as anti-inflammatory agents in inflammated connective tissue and joints and activate type II collagen synthesis [37]. Proanthocyanins are believed to alleviate clinical symptoms of pancreatitis like nausea, abdominal pain and vomiting and to slow the pathological changes that take place [38]. These compounds inhibit sensitivity of intestinal cells to insulin and inhibits α-glucosidase enzyme in the intestinal lumen thus lowering sugar levels [39]. Studies have shown that anthocyanins inhibit p53 and e-myc proapoptotic genes activity and induce the expression of Bcl-2 antiapoptotic gene [40]. Proanthocyanins and anthocyanins inhibit the activity of enzymes that induce apoptosis thus confer protective effect on cardiomyocytes after ischemic injury [[41]. Anthocyanins have been used in treatment of Epstein-Barr virus induced lymphoma, pulmonary carcinomas, gastric adenocarcinoma and ovarian carcinoma [42,43].

2. Phenolic acids

Phenolic acids are aromatic secondary plant metabolites widely spread in plants. Phenolic acids that occur naturally can divided into two main categories; cinnammic acid derivatives like ferulic acidand caffeic acid; and benzoic acid derivatives. Ferulic acid, a phenolic acid is known to have a wide range of therapeutic effect against diseases like diabetes, cancer, neurodegenerative, cardiovascular and inflammatory diseases. These therapeutic effects are believed to be attributed partly to the antioxidant activity of this phenolic acid [44]. Ferulic acid prevents lipid peroxidation and scavenges superoxide free ion radical. The structural characteristics of phenolic acids help them confer the antioxidant properties. These compounds have a phenolic nucleus and an unsaturated side chain that can form a resonance stabilized phenoxy group. Reactive radicals collide with these compounds gaining a hydrogen atom and forming a phenoxy radical [45]. Phenolic acids and their ester derivatives reduce the level of inflammatory mediators like tumor necrosis factor-alpha, prostaglandin E2

[46]. Ferulic acid also lowers the expression and inhibits function of iNOS in cells that are activated by bacterial endotoxin liposaccharide [47]. Ferulic acid derivatives have been reported to suppress the activity of cyclooxygenase-2 promoter activity in human colon cancer DLD-1 cells through the β-galactosidase reporter gene assay system [48]. Ferulic acid hydrophobic esters are reported to enhance inhibition activity of iNOS protein expression of interferon-γ/lipopolysaccharide activated RAW 264.7 cells [49].

Diabetes, an endocrine disorder is characterized by hyperglycemia leading to oxidative stress due to the over production of free radicals. Phenolic acids reduce the toxicity of streptozotocin by neutralizing the free radicals produced in the pancreas by streptozotocin [50]. The decrease in toxicity and oxidative stress in the pancreatic cells help beta cells to proliferate and secrete more insulin. Increased insulin secretion leads to decrease in glucose levels due to increased glucose utilization by extra hepatic tissues. Phenolic acids are also reported to protect proteins, DNA and lipids from oxidative stress thus exerting anticancer properties[51]. These compounds also act on pathways that regulate induction to apoptosis, response to oxidative stress and regulation of proliferation. Phenolic acids have been reported to inhibit occurrence of pulmonary cancers in mice, inhibit mutagenesis and decrease urinary N-nitrosoproline levels in humans. Phenolic compounds restore normal homeostasis by inducing apoptosis in cancer cells [52]. Phenolic acids absorb UV radiation forming a stable phenoxyl radical radiation thus terminating free radical chain reactions. These compounds preserve the physiological integrity of cells by scavenging deleterious radicals and chain reactions and suppress radiation-induced oxidative reactions [50].

Phenolic acids are believed to provide protection against polyunsaturated fatty acids (PUFA) and alcohol induced toxicity and also enables the body to overcome deleterious effects of PUFA and alcohol [51]. Phenolic acids preserve the integrity of cells exposed to alcohol stress by quenching the lipid peroxidative chain and scavenging free radicals. The mechanism of action is believed to be by abstraction of H+ by hydroperoxyl and hydroxyl radicals from a free phenolic substrate to form a phenoxyl radical which then forms products that are excreted in bile [51]. Alzheimer's, a neurodegenerative disease is characterized by free radical- mediated oxidative stress in brain cells. This oxidative stress mainly caused by reactive nitrogen species and reactive oxygen species can lead to neuronal dysfunction, RNA and DNA oxidation and lipid peroxidation. Phenolic acids are reported to prevent oxidative modification of proteins by reducing the chances of oxidative attack on them [51]. Nicotine causes oxidative cellular injury by increasing lipid peroxidation. This is believed to be a major cause of several smoking-related diseases. Phenolic acids increase the endogenous antioxidant defense system, reverses the damage caused by nicotine and protects cells from oxidative damage [50]. These compounds protect the membrane by quenching the free radicals, improve the antioxidant status and inhibit the leakage of marker enzymes into circulation.

3. Stilbenes

Stilbenes are a family of secondary metabolites derived phenylpropanoid pathway that consist a trans-ethene double bond substituted with a phenyl on both carbon atoms of the double bond. Stilbenes are believed to have anticancer properties. The mechanism of action of these compounds is inhibition of the cellular events associated with tumor initiation, promotion and progression. These compounds induces quinone reductase enzyme that plays a role in detoxifying carcinogens thus acts as an anti-mutagen [48]. Stilbenes have anti-inflammatory activities as they inhibit the arachidonic acid pathway leading to the formation of prostaglandins that activate carcinogenesis and stimulate cancer cell growth by inhibiting the hydroperoxidase activity of cyclooxygenase [49]. Stilbenes slow the progression of carcinogenesis in a dose dependent manner thus inhibits the development of preneoplastic lesions. Stilbenes are reported to inhibit DNA synthesis and duplication and lymphocyte proliferation during immunosuppressive therapies [50]. Resveratrol and ellagic acid are also known to induce apoptosis and have antiproliferative activity on human leukemia cells. Curcuminand resveratrol synergistically inhibits growth of p53- negative and p53-positive human colon cancer cells [48].

Lignans are plant polyphenolic compounds derived from phenylalanine through dimerization of substituted cinnamic acidalcohols. Lignans are known to reduce cell proliferation in colon cancer cells and to exhibit anticancer effects in *in vitro* models. These compounds inhibit of metastatic secondary tumors and decrease levels of colon cancer markers in rat models [51]. Lignans are also reported to suppress the receptor binding of platelet activating factor and inhibit the replication of human immunodeficiency virus at the integration stage. These compounds are also known to inhibit tumor necrosis factor-alpha from lipopolysaccharide-triggered murine microphage [51].

Tannins are polyphenols that are obtained from various parts of different plants belonging to multiple species. It is found in abundance in the tree bark, wood, fruit, fruit pod, leaves and roots and also in plant gall. Tannins can be classified into two broad groups – hydrolysable tannins and condensed tannins. The tannin epigallo-catechin-3-gallateis reported to exhibits anti-diabetic activity [52]. In clinical terms, all forms of tannins may participate in the management of glucose level in blood. Tannin has been shown to stimulate the receptor cells to utilize carbohydrate. Ellagic acidand quercetin act synergistically to reduce viability, proliferation and trigger apoptosis of MOLT-4 human leukemia cells [53]. Ellagic acid and resveratrol are known to effectively inhibit skin tumorgenesis in mice [54].

4. Terpenoids

Terpenoids are compounds synthesized from five carbon isoprene units mainly isopentenyl pyrophosphate and its isomer dimethylallyl pyrophosphate by terpene synthases. Terpenoids have antioxidant properties and also interact with most regulatory proteins. Plant extracts have been used both traditionally and in modern medicine in the treatment of cancer and inflammatory diseases. Terpenes are used as inhibitors of NF-kB in modern medicine [55]. NF-kB system is a cytoplasmic sensor that responds to various internal and external signals like genotoxic stress and hypoxia as well as disturbances in the immune system. NF-kB also plays a major role in the development of cellular resistance against apoptosis and anti-apoptotic signaling. Most terpenes in plants occur as terpene derivatives (terpenoids). Sesquiterpenoids are the main tepernes and are known to have NF-kB signaling inhibitory effect while triterpenoids and diterpenoids are also believed to have several potent inhibitors of NF-kB signaling system [56]. Aucubin,a monoterpenoid that occurs in plants as a glycoside derivative prevents the nuclear translocation of P65 subunit of NF-kB complex in stimulated mast cells and also inhibits the degradation of IkBa protein [56]. Previous studies also show that aucubin and linaloolhas antitumor activity plays a protective role against hepatotoxicity and as it has anti- inflammatory activity. Limonene and its derivative perillyl alcohol are believed to have inhibitory effect on pancreatic and mammary tumors

[57]. These two compounds are also known to inhibit proliferation and metastasis of gastric cancer. α-Pinene , a terpene extracted from confer trees is known to inhibit translocation of NF-kB or p65 protein into nuclei of LPS- stimulated THP-1 cells [58]. Helenalin A, a sesquiterpene inhibits DNA binding of NF-kB and the transcription of NF- kB-dependent genes by alkylating the p65 subunits of NF-kB complex [56,57]. Artemisinin, a lactone extracted from *Artemisia annua* is mainly used as an anti-malarial drug but it is also used as an antifungal, anticancer, immunosuppressive and antiangiogenesis properties [57,58].

Terpenoids also improve the skin tone, increases the concentration of antioxidants in wounds, and restore inflammed tissues by increasing blood supply [59,60]. Terpenoids also improve lung function [61]. The leaves and seeds of *S. spectabilis* are used in the treatment of diabetes due to the presence phytochemicals including terpenoids [62]. Terpenoids have shown to reduce diastolic blood pressure and lower the sugar level in blood in hypertensive and diabetic patients respectively [62]. The anthraquiononein the plant extracts of *Polygonum multiflorum* have been used in the management of peripheral neuropathy, a complication associated with diabetes mellitus [63].

5. Alkaloids

Alkaloids are phytochemicals that contain nitrogen and are derived from various amino acids. Alkaloids are known to have blood glucose lowering activity. Alkaloids tetrandineand berberine have been reported to demonstrate antioxidant activity responsible for various biological activities associated with this plant including antidiabetic activity [57]. Alkaloid fractions have shown hypoglycemic potential in mice [54]. The alkaloids l-ephedrine of *Ephedra distachya* herbs have shown hypoglycemic effect in diabetic mice due to restoration and regeneration of atrophied pancreatic islets that induces the secretion of insulin [55]. Alkaloids with therapeutic effects mainly act by affecting chemical transmitters of the nervous system like dopamine, γ-aminobutyric acid, acetylcholine and serotonin. Alkaloids are also known to be anti-arrythmic effects, antihypertensive effects, anticancer and antimalarial activity [64-70].

Alkaloids are believed to have neuro-protective, cholinergic and antioxidant activities in Alzheimer's disease [71]. These compounds have memory and cognitive-enhancing activities on Alzheimer's patients. The therapeutic effect of these compounds is believed to be by restricting oxidative stress and inflammatory reactions, enhancing cholinergic transmission, elevating estrogen and other neurotropic agents and preventing β-amyloid toxicity- formation [71]. These compounds inhibit acetylcholinesterase enzyme. Inhibition of this enzyme enhances acetylcholine activity which is one of the main strategies in the management of Alzheimer's disease. Tetramethylpyrazine, an amide alkaloid and is known to elicit hypotensive effects by inhibiting platelet aggregation and vasoconstriction [72]. This alkaloid is also believed to cause inotropic and chronotropic responses on isolated atria. Tetramethylpyrazine is used in the treatment of occlusive cerebral arteriolar diseases due to its vasodilatory effects. Alkaloids have also been reported to have antimicrobial, cytotoxic and trypanocidal activity. These compounds act by intercalating DNA thus impairing replication and transcription causing frame-shift mutations [72]. Alkaloids are also believed to elicit antimicrobial and trypanocidal activity by inhibition of protein biosynthesis and by interaction with neuroreceptors [73].

6. Saponins

Saponins are plant compounds that occur either as steroid alkaloids, glycosides of triterpenoids or steroids. These phytochemicals are known to have hypocholesterolaemic, immunostimulant, hypoglycemic effect and anticarcinogenic properties [74]. The hypoglycemic effect of saponins is believed to due to stimulation of pancreatic β-cells, inhibition of glucose transport across the brush border cells of the small intestines and suppression of transfer of glucose from the stomach to the small intestines. Saponins are also reported to inhibit gastric emptying in a dose dependent manner [75]. Saponins lower cholesterol level by forming large micelles that are then excreted in bile. These compounds are said to lower serum levels of low density lipoproteins-cholesterol and decrease absorption of cholesterol in the intestines [76].

Saponins are believed to act as adjuvants in enhancing antibody production and in the stimulation of cell mediated immune system. These compounds are reported to interact with antigen-presenting cells and induce interferon and interleukin production thus mediating immunostimulant effects [72]. Saponins inhibit tumor cell growth by apoptosis in leukemia cell line and by cell cycle arrest in breast cancer cell line [69]. They also exert antiproliferative active to prostate carcinoma cells by inducing apoptosis and cell cycle arrest at G1 phase. Saponins induce apoptosis by stimulation of cytochrome c-caspase pathway. The structure of the sugar portion in saponins influences the tumor specificity of cytotoxic action.

Saponins are believed to lower the risk of cancer and other chronic diseases. These compounds are effective for both hormone dependent and non-hormone dependent cancer [77]. Saponins are also believed to antifungal and hypocholesterolemic effects. These effects are believed to be due to combination with bile acids to form micellar aggregates. Saponins prevent hyperlipemia and liver injury induced by lipid peroxidation [78]. The mechanism of action of these compounds in this case is through inhibition of lipid peroxide peroxidation and inhibition of lipid peroxide production. Saponins are also believed to inhibit HIV infection *in vitro in* addition to having antitumor properties. This effect can be attributed to the prevention effect of HIV-induced cell fusion but have no direct effect on reverse transcriptase activity of the virus[79]. Saponins have been reported to have superoxide scavenging effect on oxygen radicals that are implicated in the development and initiation of several diseases [80]. This pro-oxidative activity makes saponins to act as hydrogen abstractor leading to initial reaction of lipid oxidation.

7. Cardiac Glycosides

Cardiac glycosides are plant secondary metabolites that have a glycoside unit and act on the contractile action of the cardiac muscle. These compounds have been used traditionally for the treatment of cardiac arrhythmias and congestive heart failure as they increase contractile force [81]. Digitalis is the most commonly used cardiac glycoside both traditionally and in modern medicine. This glycoside contains two glycosides; digitoxinand digoxinwhose structures differ only by an extra hydroxyl group on digoxin. Cardiac glycosides act by inhibition of Na+, K+-ATPase resulting to decreased intracellular K+ ions and increased intracellular Ca2+ and Na+ ions [82]. Digitalis directly inhibits proliferation of androgen dependent and androgen independent prostate cancer cell lines by initiating apoptosis and increasing intracellular Ca2+ [83]. Studies shows inhibition of cell growth in androgen dependent prostate cancer cells by ouabain[83]. Oleandrinand bufalin have apoptotic effect on normal leukocytes [84].

Cardiac glycosides have been reported to inhibit the four genes that are overexpressed in prostate cancer cells including the inhibitors of apoptosis inhibitor survivin and transcription factors [85]. Digitoxin suppresses hypersecretion of IL8, a protein implicated in lung inflammation thus inhibiting activation of the NF-B signaling pathway in cystic fibrosis [85]. These compounds have been reported to exert cytotoxic effects in both cell lines derived in advanced cancer and normal prostate epithelial cells. Oleandrin, a glycoside derived from oleander, induces apoptosis by sustaining Ca2+ increase that precedes release of cytochrome c from mitochondrion and caspase activation. Oleandrin is also reported to cause cell arrest at G2-M phase of the cell cycle in a dose dependent manner [86]. Oleandrin ability to inhibit cell growth and tumor cell proliferation is believed to be due to inhibition of the up-regulation of pERK and pAkt formation [86].

8. Sterols

Phytosterols are subgroup of steroids that have structures and functions similar to cholesterol. Phytosterols in plants act as substrates for the synthesis of secondary metabolites, regulate permeability and fluidity of cell membranes and also act as biogenic precursors of growth factors [87]. Phytosterols occurs either as sterols or stanols; the saturated forms of sterols. Absorption of stanols in the intestines is lower than that of sterols resulting to lower concentrations in blood serum. Phytosterols inhibit absorption of cholesterol in the intestines. Phytosterols and cholesterol require Niemann-Pick C1-like protein for their entry in the intestine cells. Cholesterol is esterified in the enterocytes by acetyl-coenzyme A acetyltransferase-2 enzyme and are packed into chylomicrons and transported to the lymphatic system. ABC transporters pump phytosterols and non-esterified cholesterols back to the intestinal lumen. This process lowers the amount of cholesterol assimilated in the system [88]. Clinical studies have shown that phytosterol intake leads to up to 15% reduction of LDL-cholesterol [89,90]. Intake of plant stanols reduces both plant sterol and cholesterol concentrations in the serum [91]. Genetic differences in sterol metabolism and amount of phytosterols determines the effectiveness of cholesterol lowering by phytosterol supplements. Apolipoprotein E-4 homozygote persons taking supplements with phytosterols have increased cholesterol absorption capacity and thus show significant LDL-cholesterol reduction than their counterparts [92].

β-Sitosterolis the main phytosterol in plants and it is also found in human serum together with its glycoside at lower concentrations. β-sitosterol and β-sitosterol glycoside have been reported to reduce incidences of inflammatory diseases and carcinogen-induced cancer [93,94]. These compounds are also believed to have insulin releasing effect, anti-complement and antipyretic activity [94-96]. β-sitosterol and its glycoside together have immune modulating activities on non-infectious conditions like rheumatoid arthritis and allergies and chronic infectious diseases like tuberculosis and Human Papilloma Virus [97]. A mixture of the two with higher concentrations of β-sitosterol is reported to influence the proliferation of T-lymphocytes after these cells are activated by mitogens *in vitro*. However, these phytosterols are shown to increase the proliferation of TH1-type helper cells while inhibiting TH2-type helper cells. They also inhibit the secretion of IL-4 but increases the secretion of IFN-g and IL-2 [97]. This specificity towards certain T-helper cells implies that this mixture have significant modulatory and regulatory activities in conditions where enhancement of TH1-helper cell is important for the clearance of pathogens. The mixture is also reported to increase the lytic ability of natural killer cells to cancer cell lines *in vitro* [98]. β-sitosterol and its glycoside have anti-inflammatory activity as they inhibit both tumor necrosis factor alpha and interleukin-6 in a dose dependent manner.

REFERENCES (CHAPTER 1-3)

Alasalvar CM, Al-Farsi PC, Quantick F, Shahidi R, Wiktorowic Z (2005). Effect of chill storage and modified atmosphere packaging (MAP) on antioxidant activity, anthocyanins, carotenoids, phenolics and sensory quality of ready-to-eat shredded orange and purple carrots. Food Chem. 89: 69–76.

Ames BN (1989). Endogenous oxidative DNA damage, aging, and cancer. Free Radial Research Communication. 7:121–128.

Ames BN, Shigenaga MK, Hagen TM (1993). Oxidants, antioxidants, and the degenerative diseases of aging. Proceedings of the National Academy of Sciences of the United States of America. 90: 7915- 7922.

Atoui AK, Mansouri A, Boskou G, Panagiotis K (2005). Tea and herbal infusions Their antioxidant activity and phenolic profile. Food Chem. 89: 27-36.

Barcellos-Hoff MH (2005). Integrative radiation carcinogenesis interactions between cell and tissue responses to DNA damage. Seminars in Cancer Biology.15: 138-148.

Bohr VA, Taffe BG, Larminat F (1995). DNA repair, oxidative stress and aging. In R.G. Cutler, L. Packer, A. Bertram, A. Mori (Eds). Oxidative stress and aging. Switzerland, BirkhauserVerlag Basel. 1995: pp.101–110.

Burkill IH (1993). A Dictionary of the economic products of the Malay Peninsula. 3rd printing. Malaysia, Publication Unit, Ministry of Agriculture.

Burton GW, Foster DO, Perly B, Slater TF, Smith ICP, Ingold, KU (1985). Biological antioxidants. philosophical society of royal transactions of London. Series B, Biol. Sci. 311: 565-576.

Cao Jh QY (1993). Studies on the chemical constituents of the herb huanghuaren (Sida acuta Burm. f.) leaves. China Journal of Chinese Material Medicia. 18: 681-2.

Catchpole OJ, Perry NB, De Silva BMT, Grey JB, Smallfield BM (2002). Supercritical extraction of herbs I: Saw Palmetto, St John's Wort, Kava Root, and Echinacea. Journal of Supercritical Fluids. 22: 129- 138.

Crawford DR, Edbauer-Nechamen CA, Schools GP, Salmon S, Davies JM, Davies KJA (1995). Oxidant-modulated gene expression. In Davies and Ursini (Eds). The Oxygen Paradox, Italy, Kleup University press.pp. 327–335.

Cerda S, Weitzman SA (1997). Influence of oxygen radical injury on DNA methylation. Mutation Research. 386: 141–152.

Cerutti PA, Trump BF (1991). Inflammation and oxidative stress in carcinogenesis. Cancer Cells. 3: 1–7.

Chen CH, Pearson AM, Gray JI (1992). Effects of synthetic antioxidants (BHA, BHT and PG) on the mutagenicity of IQ-like compounds. Food Chem. 3: 177-183.

Dagenais GR, Marchioli R, Tognoni G, Yusuf S (2000). Beta-Carotene. vitamin C, and vitamin E and cardiovascular Diseases, Current Cardiology Reports.2: 293-299.

Dizdaroglu M, Jaruga P, Birincioglu M, Rodriguez H (2002). Free radical induced damage to DNA Mechanisms and measurement. Free Radical Biol. Med. 32: 1102–15.

Dreher D, Junod AF (1996). Role of oxygen free radicals in cancer development. European J. of Cancer. 32A: 30–8.

Edlund AS, Sundberg B, Moritz T, Sandberg GA (1995). Microscale technique for gas- chromatography mass-spectrometry measurements of pictogram amounts of indole-3-acetic-acid in plant- tissues. Plant Physiology.108: 1043–1047.

Enstrom JE, Kanim LE, Klein MA (1992). Vitamin C intake and mortality among a sample of the United States population. Epidemiology. 3: 194-202.

Eskilsson CS, Björklund E (2000). Analytical-scale microwave-assisted extraction. J. of Chromatography. 902: 227-250.

Fiehn O (2002). Metabolomics.the link between genotypes and phenotypes, Plant Molecular Biology. 48: 155–171.

Fiehn OJ, Trethewey RN, Willmitzer L (2000). Identification of uncommon plant metabolites based on calculation of elemental compositions using gas chromatography and quadrupole mass spectrometry. Analytical Chemistry. 72: 3573–3580.

Flohé RB, Frank J, Salonearn JT, Neuzil J, Zingg J, Azzi A (2002). The European perspective on vitamin E current knowledge and future research. American Journal of Clinical Nutrition. 76: 703-716.

Fraga CG, Shigenag AMK, Park JW, Degan P, Ames BN (1990). Oxida- tive damage to DNA during aging - 8-hydroxy-2'- deoxyguano-sine in rat organ DNA and urine Proceedings of National Academy of Science. 87: 4533-4537.

Fridovich I (1998). Oxygen toxicity, a radical explanation.The J. Experi-mental Biol. 201: 1203–1209.

Fridovich I (1986). Biological effects of the superoxide radical. Archives Biochemistry and Biophysics. 247: 1–11.

Goli AH, Barzegar MS, Mohammad A (2005). Antioxidant activity and total phenolic compounds of pistachio (Pistachia Vera) hullextracts. Food Chemistry. 92: 521-525.

Grigonisa D, Venskutonisa PR, Sivikb B, Sandahlb M, Eskilssonc CS (2005). Comparison of different extraction techniques for isolation of antioxidants from sweet grass (Hierochlo¨e odorata). J. Supercritical Fluids. 33:223–233.

Guarise GB, Bertucco A, Pallado P (1994). Carbon dioxide as a supercritical solvent in fatty acid refining. theory and practice. In Rizvi

S. S. H. Supercritical fluid processing of food and biomaterials, Glasgow. Lackie Academic and Professional. pp. 27-43.

Gutteridge JM (1989). Iron and oxygen. a biologically damaging mixture. Acta Paediatrica Scandinavia. 36: 78-85.

Guyton KZ, Kensler TW (1993). Oxidative mechanisms in carcinogenesis. British Medical Bulletin. 49: 523–544.

Halkes BA, Vrasidas I, Rooijer GR, Van Den B, Albert JJ, Liskamp RMJ, Pieters RJ (2002). Synthesis and biological activity of polygala- loyl-dendrimers as stable tannic acid mimics. Bioorganic and Medici- nal Chemistry Letters. 12: 1567–1570.

Halliwell B (1994). Free radicals and antioxidants free radicals, antioxidants, and human disease: curiosity, cause, or consequence?. Lancet. 344: 721-4.

Halliwell B, Gutteridge JMC (1989). Free Radicals in Biology and Medicine, 2 Ed., Clarendon, UK, Oxford science publications. pp. 22–85.

Hashimoto H, Yoda T, Kobayashi T, Young AJ. (2002). Molecular structure of carotenoids as predicted by MNDO-AMI molecular orbital calculations. J. mole. struct. 604: 125-146.

Hayek MG (2000).Dietary vitamin E improves immune function in cats. In Reinhart G. A and Carey D. P. Eds. Recent Advances in Canine and Feline Nutrition, Iams Nutrition Symposium Proceedings.

Wilmington, OH, Orange Frazer Press. 3: 555-564.

Heinerman J (1996). Heinerman's Encyclopadia of healing herbs and spices. Englewood cliffs, New Jersey, Parker publishing company. p. 425.

Hollman PCH (2001). Evidence for health effects of plant phenols: local or systemic effects?. J. Sci. Food Agric. 81: 842–852.

Huie CW (2002). A review of modern sample-preparation techniques for the extraction and analysis of medicinal plants. Analytical and Bioanalytical Chemistry. 373: 23–30.

Jaruga P, Dizdaroglu M (1996). Repair of products of oxidative DNA base damage in human cells. Nucleic Acids Research. 24:1389– 1394.

Katsunari AK, Ito I, Higashio JT (1999). Evaluation of antioxidative activity of vegetable extracts in linoleic acid emulsion and phospholipid bilayers. J. Sci. Food Agric. 979: 142010 – 2016.

Kaufmann B, Christen P (2002). Recent extraction techniques for natural products. microwave-assisted extraction and pressurized solvent extraction, Phytochemical Analysis. 13:105–113.

Kehrer JP (1993). Free-radicals as mediators of tissue-injury and disease. Critical Reviews in Toxicology. 23: 21–48.

Khundker S, Dean JR, Jones PA (1995). Comparison between solid phase extraction and supercritical fluid extraction for the determi- nation of fluconazole from animal feed. Journal of pharmaceutical and biomedical analysis.12: 1441-1447.

Lander HM, Ogiste JS, Teng KK, Novogrodsk YA (1995). p21ras as a common signaling target of reactive free radicals and cellular redox stress. The Journal of Biological Chemistry, 270: 21195–21198.

Lao RC, Shu YY, Holmes J, Chiu C (1996). Environmental sample cleaning and extraction procedures by microwave-assisted process (MAP) technol. Microchem J. 53: 99-108.

Lee JH, Choi IY, Kim IS, Kim SY, Yang ES, Park JW (2001). Protective role of superoxide dismutases against ionizing radiation in yeast. Biochemical Biophysica Acta. 1526: 91-198.

Leo MA, Lieber CS (1999). Alcohol, vitamin A, and ß-carotene: adverse interactions, including hepatotoxicity and carcinogenicity. Am. J. Clin. Nut.. 69:1071-1085.

Lopaczynski W, Zeisel SH (2001). Antioxidants, programmed cell death, and cancer. Nutrition Research. 21:295-307.

Lopez-Sebastian S, Ramos E, Ibanez E, Bueno JM, Ballester L, Tabera J, Reglero G (1998). Dearomatization of antioxidant rosemary extracts by treatment with supercritical carbon dioxide. J. Agric. Food Chem.. 46:13-19.

Mc Call, MR Frei B (1999).Can antioxidant vitamins materially reduce oxidative damage in humans?. Free radical boil. med. 26: 1034– 1053.

Mikulikova L, Popov P (2001). Oxidative stress, metabolism of ethanol and alcohol-related diseases. J. Biomed. Sci. 8: 59–70.

Nessa F, Ismail Z, Mohamed N, Hakim MR, Haris M (2004). Free radical-scavenging activity of organic extracts and of pure .flavonoids of Blumea balsamifera. Food Chem. 88: 243–252.

Nguyen N, Evans DA, Frakman G (1994). Natural antioxidants produced by supercritical fluid extraction. In Rizvi, S. S. H. Super- critical fluid processing of food and biomaterials; Glasgow. Lackie, Academic and Professional.

Oomen HAPC, Grubben GJH (1998). Tropical leaf vegetables in human nutrition. Amsterdam, Royal Tropical Institute & Orphan publishing Co.

Orth HC, Rentel C, Schmidt PC (1999). Isolation, purity analysis and stability of hyperforin as a standard material from Hypericum perfora- tum L, J. The J. Pharmacy Pharmacol. 5: 193–200.

Ozel, MZ, Gogus F, Lewis AC (2003). Subcritical water extraction of essential oils from Thymbra spicata. Food Chem. 82: 381-386.

Rimm EB, Stampfer MJ, Ascherio A, Glovannucci E, Colditz GA, Rosner B, Willett W C (1993). Vitamin E consumption and the risk of coronary heart disease in men. New England J. Med. 328: 1450- 1456.

Roger MS (1999). Supercritical fluids in separation science – the dreams, the reality and the future J. Chromat. 856: 83-115.

Rostagno MA, Palma M, Barroso CG (2004) Pressurized liquid extraction of isoflavones from soybeans. Analytica Chimica Acta. 522: 169-177.

Sang SC, Stark RE, Rosen RT, Yang CS, Ho CT (2002). Chemical studies on antioxidant mechanism of tea catechins: analysis of radical reaction products of catechin and epicatechin with 2,2-diphenyl-1- picrylhydrazyl. Bioorgan. Med. Chem. 10: 2233-7.

Sargenti SR, Mcnair HM (1998). Comparison of solid-phase extraction and supercritical fluid extraction for extraction of polycyclic aromatic hydrocarbons from drinking water. Journal of Microcolumn Separa- tions. 10: 1125 – 131.

Shigenaga KK, Tory MH, Bruce NA (1994). Oxidative damage and mito- chondrial decay in ageing. Proceedings of National Science Aca- demy. 91: 10771-10778.

Shu YY, Ko MY, Chang YS (2003). Microwave-assisted extraction of ginsenosides from ginseng root Microchem. J. 74:131-139

Sian BA (2003). Dietary antioxidants—past, present and future? Trends in Food Sci. Technol. 14: 93-98.

Somchit BN, Reezal I, Nur V, Mutalib AR (2003). In vitro antimicro- bial activity of ethanol and water extracts of Cassia alata. J. Ethnopharmacol. 84: 1-4.

Tekel J, Hatrik S (1996). Review Pesticide residue analyses in plant material by chromatographic methods: clean-up procedures and selective detectors. J. Chromat. A. 754: 397-410.

Timothy WM, Charles DJ, David MB (2003). Reaction of OH_ radicals with H2 in sub-critical water Chemical Physics Letters. 7:144–149.

• 70 •

REFERENCES (CHAPTER 4)

1. Keinan-BL, Peeters PH, Mulligan AA, Navarro C, Slimani N, Mattisson I, *et al.* Soy product consumption in 10 European countries: The european prospective investigation into cancer and nutrition (EPIC) study. Public Health Nutr 2002;5:1217-26.
2. Lindsay SH, Claywell LG. Considering soy: Its estrogenic effects may protect women. AWHONN Lifelines 1998;2:41-4.
3. Dudek SG. Nutrition essentials for nursing practice. 4th ed. Philadelphia: Lippincott Williams and Wilkins; 2001.
4. Montgomery KS. Soy Protein. J Perinat Educ 2003;12:42-5.
5. Sacks FM, Lichtenstein A, Van Horn L, Harris W, Kris-Etherton P, Winston M: American Heart Association Nutrition Committee. Soy protein, isoflavones, and cardiovascular health. An American Heart Association Science Advisory for professionals from the Nutrition Committee. Circulation 2006;113:1034-44.
6. Anderson JW, Major AW. Pulses and lipaemia, short- and long-term effect: Potential in the prevention of cardiovascular disease. Br J Nutr 2002;88:263-71.
7. Arliss RM, Biermann CA. Does soy isoflavones lower cholesterol, inhibit atherosclerosis, and play a role in cancer prevention? Holist Nurs Pract 2002;16:40-8.
8. Hasler CM. The cardiovascular effects of soy products. J Cardiovasc Nurs 2002;16:50-63. quiz 75-6.
9. Wardlaw GM. Contemporary nutrition. 4th ed. Boston: McGraw Hill.2000
10. Taku K, Umegaki K, Sato Y, Taki Y, Endoh K, Watanabe S. Soy isoflavones lower serum total and LDL cholesterol in humans: A meta-analysis of 11 randomized controlled trials. Am J Clin Nutr 2007;85:1148-56.
11. Polini N, Rauschemberger MB, Mendiberri J, Selles J, Massheimer V. Effect of genistein and raloxifene on vascular dependent platelet aggregation. Mol Cell Endocrinol 2007;267:55-62. Epub 2006 Dec 21.
12. He J, Wofford MR, Reynolds K, Chen J, Chen CS, Myers L. *et al.* Effect of dietary protein supplementation on blood pressure A randomized, controlled trial. circulation 2011;124:589-95.
13. Whitney EN, Rolfes SR. Understanding nutrition. 9th ed. Belmont, CA: Wadsworth; 2002.

14. Adlercreutz H. Phyto-oestrogens and cancer. Lancet Oncol 2002;3:364-73.

15. Jenkins DJ, Kendall CW, D'Costa MA, Jackson CJ, Vidgen E, Singer W,*et al.* Soybean consumption and phytoestrogens: Effect on serum prostate specific antigen when blood lipids and oxidized low-density lipoprotein are reduced in hyperlipidemic men. J Urol 2003;169:507-11.

16. Adlercreutz H, Mazur W, Bartels P, Elomaa V, Watanabe S, Wähälä K,*et al.* Phytoestrogens and prostate disease. J Nutr 2000;130:658S-9S.

1. Messina MJ. Legumes and soybeans: Overview of their nutritional profiles and health effects. Am J Clin Nutr 1999;70:439S-50S.

2. Davies MJ, Bowey EA, Adlercreutz H, Rowland IA, Rumsby PC. Effects of soybean or rye supplementation of high-fat diets on colon tumour development in azoxymethane-treated rats. Carcinogenesis 1999;20:927-31.

3. Kushi LH, Meyer KM, Jacobs DR Jr. Cereals, legumes, and chronic disease risk reduction: Evidence from epidemiologic studies. Am J Clin Nutr 1999;70:451S-58S.

4. Rubio MA. Implicaciones de la fibra en distintas patologías. Nutr Hosp 2002;17:17-29.

5. Guillon F, Champ MM. Carbohydrate fractions of legumes: Uses in human nutrition and potential for health. Br J Nutr 2002;88:S293-306.

6. García Peris P, Velasco Gimeno C. Evolucion en el conocimiento de la fibra. Nutr Hosp 2007;22:20-5.

7. Edwards CA, Parrett AM. Plant cell wall polysaccharides, gums and hydrocolloids: Nutritional Aspects. In Carbohydrates in foods. Marcel Dekker Inc: New York USA; 1996. p. 319-346.

8. Trock BJ, Hilakivi-Clarke L, Clarke R. Meta-analysis of soybean Intake and breast cancer risk. J Natl Cancer Inst 2006;98:459-71.

9. Morrison G, Hark L. Medical nutrition and disease. 2nd ed. Malden,MA: Blackwell Science.inc;1999

10. Somer E. Nutrition for a healthy pregnancy. 2nd ed. New York: Henry Holt and Company.2002

11. Bhathena SJ, Velasquez MT. Beneficial role of dietary phytoestrogens in obesity and diabetes. Am J Clin Nutr 2002;76:1191-201.

12. Anderson JJ, Chen X, Boass A, Symons M, Kohlmeier M, Renner JB *et al.* Soy isoflavones: No effects on bone mineral content and bone mineral density in healthy, menstruating young adult women after one year. J Am

Coll Nutr 2002;21:388-93.

13. Holt S, Muntyan I, Likver L. Soya-Based diets for diabetes Mellitus. Alternative and Complementary Therapies. March/April 1996

14. Jenkins DJ, Kendall CW, Marchie A, Jenkins AL, Augustin LS, Ludwig DS, *et al.* Type 2 diabetes and vegetarian diet. Am J Clin Nutr 2003;78:610S-16S.

15. Chandalia M, Garg A, Lutjohann D, Von Bergmann K, Grundy SM, Brinkley LJ. Beneficial effects of high dietary fiber intake in patients with type 2 Diabetes Mellitus. N Engl J Med 2000;342:1392-8.

16. Messina MJ. In The Simple Soybean and Your Health. New York: Avery Publishing Group; 1994. p. 150-151.

17. Farriol M, Jorda M, Delgado G. Past and current trends supplementation: A bibliographic study. Nutr Hosp 2006;21:448-51.

18. Brown EC, DiSilvestro RA, Babaknia A, Devor ST. Soy versus whey protein bars: Effects on exercise training impact on lean body mass and antioxidant status. Nut J 2004;3:22.

19. Food labeling: Health claims; soy protein and coronary heart disease. Food and Drug Administration, HHS: Final rule. Fed Reg 1999;64:5770033.

20. Food and Drug Administration (FDA). FDA approves new health claim for soybean protein and coronary heart disease. FDA Talk Paper 1999, in www.fda.gov Soja, fuente de salud Nutr Hosp 2008;23:305-312.

21. Henkel J. Soybean: Health claims for soybean protein, questions about other components. FDA Consumer 2000, in www.cfsan.fda.gov2

22. Anderson JW, Johnstone BM, Cook-Newell ME. Metaanalysis of the effects of soybean protein intake on serum lipids. N Engl J Med 1995;333:276-82.

23. Reynolds K, Chin A, Lees KA, Nguyen A, Bujnowski D, He J. A Meta-analysis of the effect of soybean protein supplementation on serum lipids. Am J Cardiol 2006;98:633-40.

24. Liu KS. Chemistry and nutritional value of soybean components. In: Soybeans: Chemistry, Technology and Utilization. Gaithersburg, Maryland, USA: Aspen Publ. Inc.; 1999. p. 25-113.

25. Bosaeus I. Fiber effects on intestinal functions (diarrhoea, constipation and irritable bowel syndrome). Clin Nutr Suppl 2004;1:33-8.

26. Scheppach W, Luethrs H, Melcher R, Gostner A, Schauber J, Kudlich, T, *et al.* Antiinflammatory and anticarcinogenic effects of dietary fiber. Clin Nutr Supp 2004; 1:51-8.

27. Asif M. The role of fruits, vegetables, and spices in diabetes. Int J Nutr Pharm Neurol Dis 2011;1:27-35.

REFERENCES (CHAPTER 5)

1. Arika WM, Abdirahman YA, Mawia MA, Wambua KF, Nyamai DW. *In Vivo* Antidiabetic Activity of the Aqueous Leaf Extract of *Croton macrostachyus* in Alloxan Induced Diabetic Mice. Pharmceutica Analytica Acta. 2015; 6: 447.

2. World Health Organization (2002) WHO traditional medicine strategy 2002-2005.

3. Piero NM, Njagi MJ, Kibiti MC, Ngeranwa JJN, Njagi NM, et al. Herbal management of diabetes mellitus: A rapidly expanding research avenue. International Journal of Current Pharmaceutical Research. 2012; 4: 1-4.

4. Ali AA, Alqurainy F. Activities of antioxidants in plants under environmental stress. The lutein-prevention and treatment for diseases. 2006; 187-256.

5. Andre CM, Larondelle Y, Evers D. Dietary antioxidants and oxidative stress from a human and plant perspective: a review. Current Nutrition & Food Science. 2010; 6(1): 2-12.

6. Holst B, Williamson G. Nutrients and phytochemicals: from bioavailability to bioefficacy beyond antioxidants. Current opinion in biotechnology. 2008; 19: 73-82.

7. Piero NM, Kimuni NS, Ngeranwa JJN, Orinda GO, Njagi JM, et al. Antidiabetic and Safety of *Lantana rhodesiensis* in Alloxan Induced Diabetic Rats. Journal of Developing Drugs. 2015; 4: 129.

8. Nyamai DW, Mawia AM, Wambua FK, Njoroge A, Matheri F. Phytochemical Profile of *Prunus africana* Stem Bark from Kenya. Journal of Pharmacognosy & Natural Products. 2015; 1: 110.

9. Muriithi NJ, Maina GS, Maina MB, Kiambi MJ, Juma KK, et al. Determination of Hematological Effects of Methanolic Leaf Extract of *Vernonia lasiopus* in Normal Mice. Journal of Blood &Lymph. 2015; 5: 139.

10. Abdirahman YA, Juma KK, Mukundi MJ, Gitahi SM, Agyirifo DS. In-Vivo Antidiabetic Activity and Safety of The Aqueous Stem Bark Extract of *Kleinia squarrosa*. Journal of Diabetes & Metabolism. 2015;6: 601.

11. Mukundi MJ, Mwaniki NEN, Piero NM, Murugi NJ, Daniel AS. In Vivo Anti-diabetic Effects of Aqueous Leaf Extracts of *Rhoicissus tridentata* in Alloxan Induced Diabetic Mice. Journal of Developing Drugs. 2015; 4: 2.

12. Arika WM, Abdirahman YA, Mawia MM, Wambua KF, Nyamai DM.

Hypoglycemic Effect of *Lippia javanica* in Alloxan Induced Diabetic Mice. Journal of Diabetes & Metabolism. 2015; 6: 2.

13. Middleton E, Kandaswami C, Theoharides TC. The effects of plant flavonoids on mammalian cells: implications for inflammation, heart disease, and cancer. Pharmacological reviews. 2000; 52: 673-751.

14. Wagner KH, Elmadfa I. Biological relevance of terpenoids. Overview focusing on mono-, di- and tetraterpenes. *Annals of Nutrition & Metabolism.* 2003; 47: 95-106.

15. Romani A, Coinu R, Carta S, Pinelli P, Galardi C, et al. Evaluation of antioxidant effect of different extracts of *Myrtus communis* L. *Free Radical Research.* 2004; 38: 97-103.

16. Wang MW, Hao X, Chen K. Biological screening of natural products and drug innovation in China. Philosophical Transactions of the Royal Society B. *Biological Sciences.* 2007; 362: 1093-1105.

17. Mohammad RM, Banerjee S, Li Y, Aboukameel A, Kucuk O, et al. Cisplatin-induced antitumor activity is potentiated by the soy isoflavone genistein in BxPC-3 pancreatic tumor xenografts. *Cancer.* 2006; 106: 1260-1268.

18. Sharma V, Hupp CD, Tepe JJ. Enhancement of Chemotherapeutic Efficacy by Small Molecule Inhibition of NF-κ B and Checkpoint Kinases. *CurrentMedicinalChemistry.*2007;14: 1061-1074.Mertens-Talcott SU, Talcott ST, Percival SS. Low Concentrations of Quercetin and Ellagic Acid Synergistically Influence Proliferation, Cytotoxicity and Apoptosis in MOLT-4 Human Leukemia Cells. *The Journal of nutrition.* 2003; 133: 2669-2674.

19. Hwang JT, Ha J, Park OJ. Combination of 5-fluorouracil and genistein induces apoptosis synergistically in chemo-resistant cancer cells through the modulation of AMPK and COX-2 signaling pathways. *Biochemical and Biophysical Research Communications.* 2005; 332: 433-440.

20. Sánchez Y, Amrán D, Fernández C, de Blas E, Aller P. Genistein selectively potentiates arsenic trioxide-induced apoptosis in human leukemia cells via reactive oxygen species generation and activation of reactive oxygen species-inducible protein kinases (p38-MAPK, AMPK). *International Journal of Cancer.* 2008; 123: 1205-1214.

21. Jiang H, Ma Y, Chen X, Pan S, Sun B, et al. Genistein synergizes with arsenic trioxide to suppress human hepatocellular carcinoma. *Cancer Science.* 2010; 101: 975-983.

22. Lim HA, Kim JH, Kim JH, Sung MK, Kim MK, et al. Genistein induces

glucose-regulated protein 78 in mammary tumor cells. *Journal of Medicinal Food.* 2006; 9: 28-32.

23. Mohammad RM, Banerjee S, Li Y, Aboukameel A, Kucuk O, et al. Cisplatin-induced antitumor activity is potentiated by the soy isoflavone genistein in BxPC-3 pancreatic tumor xenografts. *Cancer.* 2006; 106: 1260-1268.

24. Majumdar AP, Banerjee S, Nautiyal J, Patel BB, Patel V, et al. Curcumin synergizes with resveratrol to inhibit colon cancer.*Nutrition and Cancer.* 2009; 61: 544-553.

25. Kuhar M, Imran S, Singh N. Curcumin and quercetin combined with cisplatin to induce apoptosis in human laryngeal carcinoma Hep-2 cells through the mitochondrial pathway. *Journal of Cancer Molecules.* 2007; 3: 121-128.

26. Zhang Y, Seeram NP, Lee R, Feng L, Heber D. Isolation and identification of strawberry phenolics with antioxidant and human cancer cell antiproliferative properties. *JournalofAgriculturalandFoodChemistry.*2008; 56: 670-675.

27. Seeram NP, Adams LS, Zhang Y, Lee R, Sand D, et al. Blackberry, black raspberry, blueberry, cranberry, red raspberry, and strawberry extracts inhibit growth and stimulate apoptosis of human cancer cells in vitro. *Journal of Agricultural and Food Chemistry.* 2006; 54: 9329-9339.

28. Benkhayal FA, Musbah EG, Ramesh S, Dhayabaran D. Biochemical studies on the effect of phenolic compounds extracted from Myrtus communis in diabetic rats. *Tamilnadu Journal of Vetenary & Animal Sciences.* 2009; 5: 87-93.

29. Yang JY, Della-Fera MA, Rayalam S, Ambati S, Hartzell D L, et al. Enhanced inhibition of adipogenesis and induction of apoptosis in 3T3-L1 adipocytes with combinations of resveratrol and quercetin. *LifeSciences.*2008;82: 1032-1039.

30. Ngugi MP, Njagi JM, Kibiti CM, Miriti PM. Pharmacological Management of Diabetes Mellitus. *Asian Journal of Biochemical and Pharmaceutical Research.* 2012; 2: 375-381

31. Joseph B, Jini D. Insight into the hypoglycaemic effect of traditional Indian herbs used in the treatment of diabetes. *Research Journal of Medicinal Plant.* 2011; 5: 352-376.

32. Pataki T, Bak I, Kovacs P, Bagchi D, Das DK, et al. Grape seed proanthocyanidins improved cardiac recovery during reperfusion after ischemia in isolated rat hearts. *The American Journal of Clinical Nutrition.*

2002; 75: 894-899.

33. Pataki T, Bak I, Kovacs P, Bagchi D, Das DK, et al. Grape seed proanthocyanidins improved cardiac recovery during reperfusion after ischemia in isolated rat hearts. *The American Journal of Clinical Nutrition.* 2002; 75: 894-899.

34. Tsuda T, Horio F, Osawa T. Cyanidin 3-O-. BETA.-D-glucoside Suppresses Nitric Oxide Production during a Zymosan Treatment in Rats. *Journal of Nutritional Science and Vitaminology.* 2002; 48: 305-310.

35. Lin LC, Kuo YC, Chou CJ. Immunomodulatory Proanthocyanidins from Ecdysanthera u tilis. *Journal of Natural Products.* 2002; 65: 505-508.

36. Howell AB. Cranberry proanthocyanidins and the maintenance of urinary tract health. *Critical Reviews in Food Science and Nutrition.* 2002; 42: 273-278.

37. Knox YM, Hayashi K, Suzutani T, Ogasawara M, Yoshida I, et al. Activity of anthocyanins from fruit extract of *Ribes nigrum L.* against influenza A and B viruses. *Acta virologica.* 2000; 45: 209-215.

38. Ali BH, Mousa HM, El-Mougy S. The effect of a water extract and anthocyanins of hibiscus sabdariffa L. on paracetamol- induced hepatoxicity in rats. *Phytotherapy Research.* 2003; 17: 56-59.

39. Garbacki N, Angenot L, Bassleer C, Damas J, Tits M. Effects of prodelphinidins isolated from *Ribes nigrum* on chondrocyte metabolism and COX activity. *Naunyn-Schmiedeberg's Archives of Pharmacology.* 2002; 365: 434-441.

40. Vinson JA, Mandarano MA, Shuta DL, Bagchi M, Bagchi D. Beneficial effects of a novel IH636 grape seed proanthocyanidin extract and a niacin-bound chromium in a hamster atherosclerosis model. *Molecular and Cellular Biochemistry.* 2002; 240: 99-103.

41. Matsui T, Ebuchi S, Kobayashi M, Fukui K, Sugita K, et al. Anti-hyperglycemic effect of diacylated anthocyanin derived from *Ipomoea batatas* cultivar Ayamurasaki can be achieved through the α-glucosidase inhibitory action. *Journal of Agricultural and Food Chemistry.* 2002; 50: 7244-7248.

42. Bagchi D, Bagchi M, Stohs SJ, Ray SD, Sen CK, et al. Cellular protection with proanthocyanidins derived from grape seeds. *Annals of the New York Academy of Sciences.* 2002; 957: 260-270.

43. Joshi SS, Kuszynski CA, Bagchi D. The cellular and molecular basis of health benefits of grape seed proanthocyanidin extract. *CurrentPharmaceuticalBiotechnology.* 2001; 2: 187-200.

44. Iwase Y, Takemura Y, Ju-ichi M, Ito C, Furukawa H, et al. Inhibitory effect of flavonoids from Citrus plants on Epstein-Barr virus activation and two-stage carcinogenesis of skin tumors. *Cancer Letters.* 2000; 154: 101-105.

45. Appendino G, Maxia L, Bascope M, Houghton P J, Sanchez-Duffhues G, et al. A meroterpenoid NF-κB inhibitor and drimane sesquiterpenoids from asafetida. *JournalofNaturalProducts.*2006; 69: 1101-1104.

46. Srinivasan M, Sudheer AR, Menon VP. Ferulic acid: therapeutic potential through its antioxidant property. *Journal of Clinical Biochemistry and Nutrition.* 2007; 40: 92.

47. Ronchetti D, Impagnatiello F, Guzzetta M, Gasparini L, Borgatti M, et al. Modulation of iNOS expression by a nitric oxide- releasing derivative of the natural antioxidant ferulic acid in activated RAW 264.7 macrophages. *European Journal of Pharmacology.* 2006; 532: 162-169.

48. Dai J, Mumper RJ. Plant phenolics: extraction, analysis and their antioxidant and anticancer properties. *Molecules.* 2010; 15: 7313-7352.

49. Uttara B, Singh AV, Zamboni P, Mahajan RT. Oxidative stress and neurodegenerative diseases: a review of upstream and downstream antioxidant therapeutic options. *Current Neuropharmacology.* 2009; 7: 65.

50. Delmas D, Lançon A, Colin D, Jannin B, Latruffe N. Resveratrol as a chemopreventive agent: a promising molecule for fighting cancer. *Current Drug Targets.* 2006; 7: 423-442.

51. Kang NJ, Shin SH, Lee HJ, Lee KW. Polyphenols as small molecular inhibitors of signaling cascades in carcinogenesis. *Pharmacology & Therapeutics.* 2011; 130: 310-324.

52. Gao X, Xu YX, Janakiraman N, Chapman RA, Gautam SC. Immunomodulatory activity of resveratrol: suppression of lymphocyte proliferation, development of cell-mediated cytotoxicity, and cytokine production. *Biochemical Bharmacology.* 2001; 62: 1299-1308.

53. Cassidy A, Hanley B, Lamuela-Raventos RM. Isoflavones, lignans and stilbenes-origins, metabolism and potential importance to human health. *Journal of the Science of Food and Agriculture.* 2000; 80: 1044-1062.

54. Piero NM, Eliud NN, Susan KN, George OO, David NJMM, et al. In Vivo Antidiabetic Activity and Safety In Rats of *Cissampelos pareira* Traditionally Used In The Management of Diabetes Mellitus In Embu County, Kenya. *Journal of Drug Metabolism & Toxicology.* 2015; 6: 184

55. Mertens-Talcott SU, Talcott ST, Percival SS. Low Concentrations of Quercetin and Ellagic Acid Synergistically Influence Proliferation, Cytotoxicity and Apoptosis in MOLT-4 Human Leukemia Cells-.

*TheJournalofNutrition.*2003;133: 2669-2674.

56. Yang CS, Landau JM, Huang MT, Newmark HL. Inhibition of carcinogenesis by dietary polyphenolic compounds. *Annual Review of Nutrition.* 2001; 21: 381-406.

57. Salminen A, Lehtonen M, Suuronen T, Kaarniranta K, Huuskonen J. Terpenoids: natural inhibitors of NF-κB signaling with anti-inflammatory and anticancer potential. *Cellular and Molecular Life Sciences.* 2008; 65: 2979-2999.

58. Lyss G, Knorre A, Schmidt TJ, Pahl HL, Merfort I. The anti-inflammatory sesquiterpene lactone helenalin inhibits the transcription factor NF-kB by directly targeting. *Journal of Biological Chemistry.* 1998; 273: 33508-33516.

59. Aggarwal BB, Ichikawa H, Garodia P, Weerasinghe P, Sethi G, et al. From traditional Ayurvedic medicine to modern medicine: identification of therapeutic targets for suppression of inflammation and cancer. *Expert Opinion on Therapeutic Targets.* 2006; 10: 87-118

60. Mujoo K, Haridas V, Hoffmann JJ, Wächter GA, Hutter LK, et al. Triterpenoid saponins from Acacia victoriae (Bentham) decrease tumor cell proliferation and induce apoptosis. *Cancer Research.* 2001; 61: 5486-5490.

61. Grace MH, Esposito D, Dunlap KL, Lila MA. Comparative analysis of phenolic content and profile, antioxidant capacity, and anti-inflammatory bioactivity in wild Alaskan and commercial vaccinium berries. *Journal of Agricultural and Food Chemistry.* 2013; 62: 4007-4017.

62. McPartland JM, Russo EB. Cannabis and cannabis extracts: greater than the sum of their parts?. *Journal of Cannabis Therapeutics.* 2001; 1: 103-132.

63. Dholi SK, Raparla R, Mankala SK, Nagappan K. Invivo Antidiabetic evaluation of Neem leaf extract in alloxan induced rats. Journal of Applied Pharmaceutical Science. 2011; 1 : 100-105

64. Raskin J, Pritchett YL, Wang F, D'Souza DN, Waninger AL, et al. (2005) A double-blind, randomized multicenter trial comparing duloxetine with placebo in the management of diabetic peripheral neuropathic pain. *Pain Medicine,* 6: 346-356.

65. Sharma B, Salunke R, Balomajumder C, Daniel S, Roy P. Anti-diabetic potential of alkaloid rich fraction from Capparis decidua on diabetic mice. *Journal of ethnopharmacology.* 2010; 127: 457-462.

66. Abdirahman YA, Juma KK, Mukundi MJ, Gitahi SM, Agyirifo DS. The Hypoglycemic Activity and Safety of Aqueous Stem Bark Extracts of

Acacia nilotica. *Journal of Drug Metabolism Toxicology.* 2015; 6: 189-198.

67. Verma A, Yadav MR, Giridhar R, Prajapati N, Tripathi AC, et al. Nitrogen Containing Privileged Structures and their Solid Phase Combinatorial Synthesis. *Combinatorial Chemistry & High Throughput Screening.* 2013; 16: 345-393.

68. Dastmalchi K, Dorman HD, Vuorela H, Hiltunen R. Plants as potential sources for drug development against Alzheimer's disease. *International Journal of Biomedical* and *Pharmaceutical* Sciences. 2007; 1: 83-104.

69. Chiu-Yin KWAN, Achike FI. Tetrandrine and related bis-benzylisoquinoline alkaloids from medicinal herbs: cardiovascular effects and mechanisms of action. *Acta Pharmacologica Sinica.* 2002; 23: 1057-1068.

70. O'Brien P, Carrasco-Pozo C, Speisky H. Boldine and its antioxidant or health-promoting properties. *Chemico-biological interactions.* 2006; 159: 1-17.

71. Guruvayoorappan C, Sakthivel KM, Padmavathi G, Bakliwal V, Monisha J, et al. *Anticancer Properties of Fruits and Vegetables: A Scientific Review.* 2014; 1.

72. Francis G, Kerem Z, Makkar HP, Becker K. The biological action of saponins in animal systems: a review. *British Journal Of Nutrition.* 2002; 88: 587-605.

73. Ros E. Intestinal absorption of triglyceride and cholesterol. Dietary and pharmacological inhibition to reduce cardiovascular risk. *Atherosclerosis.* 2000; 151: 357-379.

74. Tan BK, Vanitha J. Immunomodulatory and antimicrobial effects of some traditional Chinese medicinal herbs: a review. Curr Med Chem. 2004; 11: 1423-1430.

75. Chung MK. Vitamins, supplements, herbal medicines, and arrhythmias. *Cardiology in Review.* 2004; 12: 73-84.

76. Hostanska K, Nisslein T, Freudenstein J, Reichling J, Saller R. Apoptosis of human prostate androgen-dependent and- independent carcinoma cells induced by an isopropanolic extract of black cohosh involves degradation of cytokeratin (CK)18. *Anticancer research.* 2005; 25: 139-147.

77. Lee KJ, Choi CY, Chung YC, Kim YS, Ryu SY, et al. Protective effect of saponins derived from roots of Platycodon grandiflorum on tert-butyl hydroperoxide-induced oxidative hepatotoxicity. *Toxicology letters.* 2004; 147: 271-282.

78. Jassim SAA, Naji MA. Novel antiviral agents: a medicinal plant

perspective. *Journal of Applied Microbiology*. 2003; 95: 412-427.

79. Zhu, YZ, Huang SH, Tan BKH, Sun J, Whiteman M, et al. Antioxidants in Chinese herbal medicines: a biochemical perspective. *Natural Product Reports*. 2004; 21: 478-489.

80. Liu J, Tian J, Haas M, Shapiro JI, Askari A, et al. Ouabain interaction with cardiac Na+/K+-ATPase initiates signal cascades independent of changes in intracellular Na+ and Ca2+ concentrations. *Journal of Biological Chemistry*. 2000; 275: 27838- 27844.

81. Yeh JY, Huang WJ, Kan SF, Wang PS. Effects of bufalin and cinobufagin on the proliferation of androgen dependent and independent prostate cancer cells. *The Prostate*. 2003; 54: 112-124.

82. Newman RA, Yang P, Pawlus AD, Block KI. Cardiac glycosides as novel cancer therapeutic agents. *Molecular Interventions*. 2008; 8: 36.

83. Pollard B. *U.S. Patent No. 8,569,248*. Washington, DC: U.S. Patent and Trademark Office. 2013.

84. Newman RA, Kondo Y, Yokoyama T, Dixon S, Cartwright C, et al. Autophagic cell death of human pancreatic tumor cells mediated by oleandrin, a lipid-soluble cardiac glycoside. *Integrative cancer therapies*. 2007; 6: 354-364.

85. Hartmann MA Plant sterols and the membrane environment. *Trends in Plant Science*. 1998; 3: 170-175.

86. Patel MD, Thompson PD. Phytosterols and vascular disease. *Atherosclerosis*. 2006; 186: 12-19.

87. Hendriks HFJ, Weststrate JA, Van Vliet T, Meijer GW. Spreads enriched with three different levels of vegetable oil sterols and the degree of cholesterol lowering in normocholesterolaemic and mildly hypercholesterolaemic subjects. *European Journal of Clinical Nutrition*. 1999; 53: 319-327.

88. Katan MB, Grundy SM, Jones P, Law M, Miettinen T, et al. Efficacy and safety of plant stanols and sterols in the management of blood cholesterol levels. In *MayoClinicProceedings*.2003; 78: 965-978.

89. O'Neill, FH, Sanders TA, Thompson GR. Comparison of efficacy of plant stanol ester and sterol ester: short-term and longer-term studies. *The American Journal of Cardiology*. 2005; 96: 29-36.

90. Vanhanen HT, Blomqvist S, Ehnholm C, Hyvönen M, Jauhiainen M, et al. Serum cholesterol, cholesterol precursors, and plant sterols in hypercholesterolemic subjects with different apoE phenotypes during dietary sitostanol ester treatment. *Journal of Lipid Research*. 1993; 34:

1535-1544.

91. Yamamoto M, Masui T, Sugiyama K, Yokota M, Nakagomi K, et al. Anti-inflammatory active constituents of Aloe arborescens Miller. *AgriculturalandBiologicalChemistry.* 1991; 55: 1627-1629.

92. Raicht RF, Cohen BI, Fazzini EP, Sarwal AN, Takahashi M. Protective effect of plant sterols against chemically induced colon tumors in rats. *Cancer Research.* 1980; 40: 403-405.

93. Ivorra MD, D'ocon MP, Paya M, Villar A. Antihyperglycemic and insulin-releasing effects of beta-sitosterol 3-beta-D-glucoside and its aglycone, beta-sitosterol. *ArchivesInternationalesDePharmacodynamieet de Thérapie.* 1987; 296: 224-231.

94. Yamada H, Yoshino M, Matsumoto T, et al. Effects of phytosterols on anti-complementary activity, *Chemical &Pharmaceutical Bulletin.* 1987; 35: 4851-4855

95. Yamada H, Yoshino M, Matsumoto T, Nagai T, Kiyohara H, et al. Effects of phytosterols on anti-complementary activity.*Chemical and Pharmaceutical Bulletin.* 1987; 35: 4851-4855.

96. Harshal, CK, Prakash SL. Comparative Studies on Antioxidant and Antipyretic Activities of Leaf Extracts of Cassia fistula,Psida cordifolia and Aegel marmelos. *Research Journal of Biotechnology.* 2014; 9: 2.

97. Bouic PJD, Etsebeth S, Liebenberg RW, Albrecht CF, Pegel K, et al. Beta-sitosterol and beta-sitosterol glucoside stimulate human peripheral blood lymphocyte proliferation: Implications for their use as an immunomodulatory vitamin combination. *International Journal of Immunopharmacology.* 1996; 18: 693-700.

ABOUT THE AUTHOR

Dr. Hilal Ahmad Punoo is working as Senior Assistant Professor in Department of Food Science and Technology University of Kashmir Srinagar J&K. He has been appointed as Assistant Professor in Department of Food Science and Technology University of Kashmir Srinagar in 2010. Dr. Hilal Ahmad Punoo has completed B.Sc. in Agriculture in 2000 from Narain college Shikohabad and M.Sc. in Agriculture (Dairy Science) in 2003 from R.B.S. college Bichpuri Agra, Agra University Uttar Pradesh. He has done Ph.D. in Dairy Technology from National Dairy Research Institute Karnal (I C A R) in 2009. He has 11 years of teaching and research experience. He has guided 75 M.Sc Students in different research projects. He is supervising 5Ph.D students. His area of research is development and fortification of fruit beverages, development and modification of soy foods, Dairy foods characterization and formulation, nutraceutical exploration of traditional foodsetc. He has 15 publications in national and International journals. He is life member of Association of Food Scientists and Technologists India, Indian Dairy Association and Dairy Technologists Society of India. He has one patent.